Bonding
with the
Blonde Women

Ellie Lofaro

LifeJourney® is an imprint of
Cook Communications Ministries, Colorado Springs, CO 80918
Cook Communications, Paris, Ontario
Kingsway Communications, Eastbourne, England

BONDING WITH THE BLONDE WOMEN

First Printing 2003
Printed in United States of America
1 2 3 4 5 6 7 8 9 10 Printing/Year 07 06 05 04 03

Editor: Janet Lee
Cover Design: Jeff Barnes

Library of Congress Cataloging-in-Publication Data Applied For

Dedication

This book is lovingly dedicated to Frank Lofaro,
my husband of 20 years.

Your encouragement, guidance, and support
has meant more than you'll ever know.

There's not a day that goes by that I don't
realize how perfect you are for me.

I am so glad I married you.

Acknowledgments

My heart felt thanks to...

My husband Frank—Honey, I'm thrilled you actually enjoy being Mr. Mom a couple of weekends a month.

Paris, Jordan, and Capri—I am crazy for you. Please stop growing so fast.

My favorite brunette Kathy Troccoli—You've reminded me that I am so much more than a housewife in suburbia. Thank you for a friendship like I've never known.

My amazing mentor Patsy Clairmont—Is it possible that you have carved out time to teach me the secrets of the universe? I've always admired the wise teacher. Little did I know I'd come to treasure the wonderful friend.

My Prayer Partners—My words touch hearts because your knees touch the ground.

The Bright Pond Bible Study—Who needs reality TV when we have each other? I absolutely love Wednesday mornings.

The Women of Faith Family—Your kindness never goes unnoticed.

Dave VanPatten—for transforming good ideas into a great plan.

Linda Anders, Lynn Griffin, Tracy Key, Chris Lopez, Susan Stinson, and Monica Sullenberger—You are God-sends one and all. Because of you, my load is so much lighter.

Janet Lee—for remaining calm, cool and Christlike in the crunch.

Cook Communications Ministries—for inviting the freshman to become a sophomore.

The Good Lord—for using me in spite of myself.

Table of Contents

Foreword
by Patsy Clairmont

Has anyone ever crossed your path that was so engaging, intelligent, and delightful that you immediately hoped they would always be your friend? That was my first response to Ellie Lofaro. I found her lively outlook, her zany humor, and her wide-open arms to people refreshing. And now that she is a regular in my life circle and we have stayed in each others homes, exchanged phone calls, and e-mails, I am convinced the strong magnetic draw to Ellie is the Lord. The sparkle in her eyes is so obviously lit by the fire of Christ in her heart. Ellie is committed to the Savior, the Scripture, and the sanctified life.

Ellie is a truth seeker as well as a truth speaker. I find that appealing. I prefer bottom line folks who know how to say what needs to be said in strength and kindness. But don't get me wrong—this incredible follower of Christ is incredibly human. But you'll figure that out in the pages ahead as you help dab the dripping hair color out of her eyes, learn why smoked turkey steams her, observe the true grit of a sand castle, and Reebok with her at breakneck-pace through her "normal" summer day. If not for Jesus, this gal, I am convinced, could be dangerous (now we see why I like her), but instead she adds dynamics to the adventurous.

And while Ellie makes me giggle color into my fair face, she also causes me to pause, ponder, and praise. If you're like me you'll want to sit a spell, absorb, and be encouraged by her White House moment, her evaluation of Real Dads, and her poignant response to The Mourning After.

I identify, and I believe you will too, with Ellie's tendencies toward life to over react one moment and under react the next; to form strong opinions only then to have those changed by God's greater counsel. And I resonate with her longing to move forward to become more like Christ.

Ellie's fragrant potpourri stories allow us all to find favorite pages we can dog-ear to share and revisit again and again. There's something for everyone: the workaholic, the frenzied mom, the passionate mate, the reluctant pet owner, the patriot, the broken-hearted, and more.

Here's my recommendation for the next time you have a beige day: pull out one of Ellie's essays and allow it to help color-in your perspective. She's a fiesta waiting for guests. Its fun to view a technicolor life and no one demonstrates that better than my witty and wondrous friend as she inspires me with her relevancy.

I've walked the halls of Ellie's primary colored home with its painted parrot, oversized Crayolas, and framed New York landscapes. I've conversed with Ellie's dashing husband Frank whom you will hear about repeatedly and whom you will find yourself applauding. And I have enjoyed the company of her exceptional children who help keep Ellie anchored and real. I've even ruffled the hair of sweet Bella. I have guffawed with Ellie, fervently prayed, and passionately shared matters of the heart, and we have bonded.

Oh, yes, and did I mention...I'm blonde.

Blessings,
Patsy

Preface
Bonding with the Blonde Women

A llow me to begin at the beginning. I was born in Brooklyn, New York, on October 17, 1957. I was named Elvira Robina Mannarino, and my parents were Albert and Alessandra. We lived on Herkimer Street off Eastern Parkway in the same brownstone where my father grew up with his ten siblings. My family moved to Long Island in the early sixties for a slice of the good life. Thanks to my three brothers, Ronald, Robert, and Richard, I was very athletic and also adept at self-defense. The fifth and final stork delivery produced my sister Michelle—the ally and friend I had always hoped for.

Although New York is often referred to as a huge melting pot, the vast majority (all, to be exact) of my childhood friends were of European ancestry. Like most sprawling suburbs across America at that time, there existed an unspoken wall of segregation. Chances of meeting African-, Asian-, South American-, or Middle Eastern-Americans were slim to none in my white, "Wonder Years" neighborhood. In 1970, we moved to a larger house on a wooded acre, and that home is the setting of my fondest memories from my middle school, high school, and college years.

Most New Yorkers never go too far from the nest. I never imagined that ten years after graduating from Boston College, I would return to the same town I grew up in, but with a husband and a baby. I embraced marriage and motherhood, and my church became very central to my life. I loved the church and I loved our pastors. I especially loved the women of the church. I admired their strength and their servant hearts. I was often convicted by their "no problem...can do" attitudes. These women took Titus 2 seriously, and they freely opened their hearts and homes. I entered both and took plenty of notes. Then in the summer of 1994, after fifteen years of "belonging," we moved away.

Moving out of state really devastated me. In the past, when I had heard women say things like that, I thought they were wimps. (Open wide, eat, and swallow hard.) It's not that I couldn't function—on the contrary, I threw myself into things full force. I was looking to belong—but there were no takers. I had always proudly proclaimed, "God is all I need." When I left everything and everyone that was familiar, I felt the Lord responding, "Really? Let's see." I later realized the lesson was not to torture me but to test me. The refiner's fire can be very painful, but it produces purity, strength, and value.

Enter "The Blonde Women." I would like to go on record to clarify that my blonde women are not the blonde women from blonde-women jokes. My blonde women are smart, sophisticated, articulate, talented, athletic, accessorized, and very thin. Those are just some of the reasons I didn't like them. Of course they didn't know that. I always made sure I sent mounds of sloppy agape in their direction. I had never encountered the blonde women until we moved to Virginia. The thing that really bugged me the most about the blonde women was that they just smiled and nodded and smiled and nodded. I could never tell what they were thinking.

I shared some of my blonde women issues a couple of years ago during a ladies luncheon at a wealthy mainline church nearby. The very blonde audience laughed heartily as I shared my frustrations, and they seemed to empathize with my difficulty adjusting. When my message ended and dessert was served (all on fine china), an elegant fifty-something blonde woman made a beeline in my direction. I prepared for the worst. She came uncharacteristically close (for a blonde woman) and declared, "Darling, being blonde is simply a matter of time and money." She winked, grinned knowingly, and walked away.

That's when it hit me. I wasn't able to bond with the blonde women because they were so very different than I was. They looked, acted, spoke, smelled, and walked differently than I did. And their names—even their names were blonde: Linda White, Susan Jones, Lisa Smith, Pam Thompson, Catherine Wilson, Kim Short. (Straight off the roster of the DAR—no relation whatsoever to Fellini.) I had spent almost four decades in settings where there was little or no diversity. I had become accustomed to my own kind (yes, even in a church body), but God had a better way.

So you see, it was never about the blonde women—it was always about me. What seemed like aloofness was actually self-control and poise. What seemed like guarded conversation was actually a well-trained tongue. What seemed like formality was a genteel civility. I was thrown into a new culture, and I made the foolish mistake of thinking that the adjustments should be made by everyone else. To top things off, their beauty and poise felt quite threatening. Jokes about health and weight were no longer funny. I began to wonder how I was perceived by the blonde women. (I put one in a headlock until she came clean.) She thought I was arrogant, opinionated, and too inquisitive. I had thought I was confident, clear thinking, and concerned. She said I was aggressive. I had thought I was assertive. She disrespected my tardiness and lack of organization. I thought I was a multitalented creative spirit out to touch the world.

I knew it was time to repent. If you don't humble yourself, the Lord has ways of doing it for you. My judgmental attitude had to go. The Lord began to show me His "severe mercy." He taught me to be slow to speak, careful to judge, and quick to forgive, and He made me more aware of my own need to be forgiven. The process has shown me the depths of His grace and boundless love. I have sincerely embraced the concept of being His workmanship, although I still squirm while I'm being worked on.

I now enjoy meaningful relationships with the blonde women (see Chapter 30 for the rest of the story)—and many others who don't "look" like me. Our senior pastor is an African American, and the church is gloriously integrated. Our suburban neighborhood is comprised of families whose ancestry can be traced to five continents. There is even a house with an opinionated, dark-haired Italian woman from New York.

B ut he said to me, "My grace is sufficient for you, for my power is made perfect in weakness." Therefore I will boast all the more gladly about my weaknesses, so that Christ's power may rest on me.
—2 Corinthians 12:9

1

The Mourning After

September 12, 2001

I t looked like something Steven Spielberg and George Lucas
whipped up in their special effects studio. Hijacked planes,
balls of flame, debris (and people) falling from burning build-
ings, skyscrapers being leveled to dust, pedestrians scrambling for
cover. Many of us have paid money to be "entertained" by such "life-
like" scenes. Disaster movies like *Towering Inferno* and *Poseidon
Adventure* were startling when they were first released on the
big screen nearly three decades ago. However, the sophisticated
technology employed in the more recent *Deep Impact* and
Independence Day make those older films seem quite benign. Box
offices around the world collected millions of dollars so audiences
could watch major cities burn in "sensurround sound." Imagine *that*.

It is Wednesday morning, September 12, 2001—and I am trying to absorb the extent of the devastation that keeps unfolding on
my television screen. As a true-blue-born-and-bred New Yorker who
has called D.C. home for the past seven years, I can't yet fathom this
disaster that has forever left its cruel mark on countless lives.
Twenty four hours ago, my world changed. I've seen "this kind of
world" in far away places, but "this kind of world" is no longer far
away. This is *my* world!

I feel perplexed. I feel sad. I feel angry. I feel sick. I feel dazed.
I feel numb. I feel attacked. These are MY cities! These are the places

where most of my family and friends work and live.

These cities are the very core of American democracy and capitalism; they directly impact the politics and finances of the entire world. These are the two cities I proudly show off to guests. We have come to love Washington and have become increasingly patriotic as we bring out-of-towners to the museums and monuments along the Mall. In New York, we have precious memories of Radio City, Rockefeller Center, Broadway musicals, South Street Seaport, and Little Italy. We have stood on the observation deck of the north tower many times with family and friends.

Frank and I dined at Windows on the World during our engagement. I remember we laughed hard when the bill came because of the thick fog that blocked the usually spectacular view. I've sat in the River Café under the Brooklyn Bridge a few times, gaping at the beauty of the Manhattan skyline so powerfully punctuated by the majestic twin towers. I recently brought a group of young women from church to their first "field trip" to The Big Apple. I was delighted by their awe and childlike wonder as we walked through the city that never sleeps. We stayed at the Marriott World Trade Center Hotel that weekend. We were there! I watch my two cities burning. What a disaster—and it's not a movie!

I wanted it to be a bad dream—an apocalyptic nightmare—but when I awoke today, my memory played back the horrific sights that left me weeping quietly for hours yesterday morning as I sat alone in the house. There is no delete button I can press to undo the dark deeds done in New York, Pennsylvania, and D.C. I am convinced the sights and sounds of the past twenty four hours will remain with me forever. And *that's* not an entirely bad thing. I need to remember. I must not forget.

There was a time when the only cities on fire were far across the ocean. I review mental images of Belfast, Beirut, and Kosovo, and I wonder how I managed to compartmentalize my emotions. My stomach has been in a knot, and I think about mothers in those "other worlds" where war is unrelenting. It is suddenly all so personal. The President has just announced that war has been declared on America and that the evildoers will be punished. The word "evil" is all over the news. I am trying to comprehend the enormity of it, put a face on it, and figure out what my role in the battle should be.

We live twenty minutes from the Pentagon and just ten minutes from Dulles Airport. School is fittingly cancelled today. My 9-year-old and my 12-year-old are content to enjoy a "free" day. Frank has gone to work, to lead devotions at Prison Fellowship, and I watched some early morning reports. My 14-year-old sits next to me on the couch, much closer than usual. Some of the names now have faces, and there are stories of good-byes that would unknowingly be final. I have nothing to add to the testimonies, sobs, and pleas of loved ones—so I don't.

The horror continues as the pall of smoke and ash hangs over Manhattan. The mighty five-walled fortress which houses our greatest warriors looks sadly deflated. I have just turned the television off and sent the three kids to a neighbor's pool. On the way, I learn that Capri's schoolmate lost her grandparents on the plane which tore into the Pentagon. Jordan's schoolmate's dad was killed there. This tragedy is too close—it's getting too personal. To quote an overwhelmed, teary-eyed firefighter, "It's just *too* much."

Now it is noon and the house is quiet and I am left alone once again with a wide array of emotions—and gut-wrenching images still stuck on replay keep flashing in my mind. I need refuge and relief for my aching heart. I turn to Psalms 23, 46, and 91, and I am genuinely comforted. I fix my eyes, my mind, and my heart upon the Lord. He knows my comings and goings and is aware of all my days. He is also the keeper of my husband and children. He is a mighty God, and His power transcends human comprehension. He is a kind God, and His love is far greater than any hatred. He is a just God, and He will balance the scales in His time.

The Bible is FULL of specific marching orders for those willing to follow in times like these:

Psalm 49—*My mouth will speak words of wisdom, my heart will give under-standing, and I will turn my ear to a proverb. Why should I fear when evil days come?*

Psalm 50—*I will call upon God in the day of trouble and He will deliver me and He will honor me. In Him alone I will put my trust.*

Psalm 51—*I will teach transgressors God's ways and they will turn back to Him.*

Micah 6—*I must act justly and love mercy and walk humbly with my God.*

Ephesians 5—*I need to be very careful how I live—not as unwise but as wise, making the most of every opportunity, because the days are evil.*

Romans 12—*I shall hate what is evil and cling to what is good. I will be devoted and honor others above myself.*

Tonight the kids will go to youth group as they do every Wednesday night. We'll stay close to home for a while and linger at the altar this Sunday. Then we'll resume our travel schedule next week. Paris will fly to New York to attend a conference where high school students will be equipped to impact their generation with the gospel. Frank will fly to Colorado to further the network of Prison Fellowship's Angel Tree Project. And I will fly to Pennsylvania to speak at a women's retreat.

In the meantime, we'll fly our flag, mourn the loss of so many and so much, and offer our heartfelt prayers. But we will not fear. The steel and glass of the magnificent twin towers have crumbled, but the strong foundations are still intact. They were strong and secure. Because of Jesus, so are mine.

He will be the sure foundation for your times, a rich store of salvation and wisdom and knowledge; the fear of the LORD is the key to this treasure.

—Isaiah 33:6

2

A Beautiful Day in the Neighborhood

When the phone rang, I did what I always do—I checked the caller ID. It was 3 P.M., and I was busy typing my notes for an upcoming women's conference in Philadelphia. The topic was JOY, and I wasn't feeling too much of it on that particular Friday in September. It was the close of week two of the new school year. And what a week it was.

The caller ID (my trusted friend), indicated the caller was Fairfax County Public Schools. That can't all fit in the little screen, so it actually said FAIRFAX COUNT PUB. At the time, Capri was a fourth grader at the public elementary school. Jordan was a seventh grader at the public middle school. Paris was a ninth grader at the public high school. So, whenever the caller ID says FAIRFAX COUNTY PUB, I do what any good mother would do. I pick up.

"Hello?"

A pause, a clicking sound, and then a saccharin, yet melodic voice comes on the line.

"Hello, this is Mrs. Leslie, Principal of Herndon High School." I was about to greet her and exchange polite formalities, when I suddenly realized that Mrs. Leslie was talking. She kept talking. And talking. And talking. It was a recording! I was the audience! And she kept talking! I laughed out loud before deciding to pay close attention to her mass-marketing message:

I am calling to let you know that in light of the recent ter-rorist attacks, we have had a good week here at Herndon High School. I am proud of our students and their behavior has been exemplary. You, too, can be proud of your child. The schedule has gone uninterrupted and the hallway traffic has moved smoothly with no incidents. The students have shown respect and kindness to all fellow students. Their safety is of utmost concern and we have increased the visibility of security and teaching staff. I want to congratulate you, as parents, for the fine job you are doing in raising these wonderful young adults. It is our privilege to lead them into the 21st century. Have a restful weekend.

Click ...

What did she mean? Was she pleased there were no riots? Or that the students went to class on time? Or that there were no food fights between the jocks and the nerds? The Republicans and the Democrats? Since when was hallway traffic moving smoothly a cause for celebration? What was the alternative? A student council led sit-in? I reflected upon Mrs. Leslie's sincere effort and wondered about her sweeping accolades of praise for the students and parents. Maybe I was missing something ...

Fast forward four weeks to my first "Homecoming Day" in 22 years. At my last one, the mighty Boston College Eagles defeated West Point. I have wonderful memories of the New England foliage, the crisp air, the new sweaters, the marching band, the hot dogs and warm pretzels. And there's nothing like a tailgate party with good friends. Who knew college life was so carefree? Ah, the good old days.

But this homecoming would be a first in many ways. The section of Reston in which we live is zoned for the secondary schools in the neighboring town of Herndon. Reston and Herndon border one another and that's where their commonality ends. Reston is a planned community, 32 years old, contemporary, and named for Robert E. Simon, a new-age entrepreneur. It is booming with high-tech industry. Herndon is an incorporated town with a mayor and a private police force. It is 145 years old, historic, and named for Naval Commander William Herndon. Yep, there's something for everyone in these here parts.

Jordan was to march in the Herndon Town Parade with his shiny new trombone. We rushed to the sidewalk in front of town hall at 9 A.M. and waited anxiously for the Herndon Middle School Marching Band to pass by. I had never been to a small town parade. I've been to the Macy's parade and one for the Yankees. Not quite the same. Boy Scouts and Girl Scouts and class floats and athletes and princesses and firemen and police officers on bikes, and the high school band and the school clubs marched along. Political candidates—both local and statewide—shook hands, distributing bumper stickers and kissing babies. There wasn't anything spectacular about this parade. It wasn't going to appear on the evening news. It seemed loosely organized—but I'll never forget it.

Hundreds of little American flags waved vigorously. The garbage truck, the fire truck, the highway department truck, and the postal truck all displayed much larger flags, and each was met with loud cheers. And finally, the middle school band passed by. The moisture on my face wasn't just from the rainy drizzle that was falling. Our boy looked like a young man, and the atmosphere prompted me to consider the sad reality that he might one day be called to march to the defense of his country.

The kickoff was at 1:30, but we got to the field at 1 to watch the pre-game festivities. The clouds had passed and the sky was electric blue. The high school and middle school marching bands took the field and played "The Star-Spangled Banner," and everyone over 30 was crying. There was emotion, devotion, patriotism, and resolve on every face. They then played "America, the Beautiful," and it surely was on that crisp fall afternoon. All stood. All sang. All remembered.

As we sat together on the bleachers as a family, the sights, sounds, and smells took me right back to my high school days. In my senior year at Half Hollow Hills High School, I lost the Homecoming Queenship by seven votes. I later learned that interesting detail through a close friend who happened to be the student council treasurer, in charge of counting—and recounting—all the ballots.

If, in the course of the year, the Queen died or was unable to fulfill her duties for any reason, I would be the one to step in and take her place. The committee never called.

I have put it all behind me, and I am not bitter.

The Herndon High School Homecoming Dance was held that evening, and it would be a first for our precious Paris and her friends. Robyn's mom would drop them off, and I was to pick them up at midnight—but I'm growing older and cannot stay awake. I got there at 11:30. Having spent 10 years teaching at a public high school, I confidently enter in without hesitation. The rest of the parents waited in their cars. How great it felt when Paris broke away from a large circle to greet me with a hug and a cheerful "Hi Mommy!" Again, the moment was not lost as I realized she had become a young woman. What would the future of America have in store for this great kid? Only the Lord knows.

My carpool duties fulfilled, I returned home in time to kiss Capri good night. She is short and skinny and very much still a child, but I know that she, too, will grow and go. I am so thankful for these years with them.

As I fell asleep that night, I reflected on the cheerleader-like phone call from the principal. Maybe the behavior of many students really has been exemplary. Maybe many parents are actually doing a good job as they attempt to raise wonderful young adults. Maybe we have all been given a wake-up-call as we lead our children into the 21st century. Maybe.

The greatest Homecoming Day of all awaits those who put their hope in God. I'll be there. I'll be marching in that parade and shouting out every song and cheering as the Homecoming King passes by on Main Street of the New Jerusalem. We may not know what the future holds—for us or for our children—but we can know the One Who holds the future. He has promised us a Homecoming Day. It will be glorious, and it will be such a relief to finally be home.

T hey will make war against the Lamb, but the Lamb will overcome them because he is Lord of lords and King of kings—and with him will be his called, chosen and faithful followers.

—Revelation 17:14

3

A Good Name

Eight weeks of media coverage had not readied me for my first trip to New York following the terror of September 11. As the USAir shuttle headed north from Reagan to Laguardia, I remember asking the flight attendant which side of the plane would provide the best view of Manhattan. I knew logically what I would see—but I was stunned emotionally by what I could no longer see. How could those towers have vanished? How could the landscape of thirty years be so brutally altered in thirty minutes? How could such enormous devastation be incurred by such hateful cowards? The sight was a painful one, and my teary eyes looked away after several minutes. The sick feeling I had experienced eight weeks earlier as I watched the horror of 9/11 unfold on television had suddenly returned. The view from the sky over NY was shocking to my senses and truly beyond my ability to comprehend.

No theology, philosophy, or sociology course had prepared me for this. I *did* take a history course once on World War II. I was 18. Maybe I should have paid more attention when we covered the Holocaust. The professor mentioned the number "six million" on a frequent basis, as well as the words "never forget." When I was 22 I visited Dachau on a backpacking trek across Europe, and that number and those words took on more meaning.

Now I'm 44. Seeing the New York skyline so changed suddenly

made the words "never forget" more poignant and powerful than ever before. The terrorism on America left *a lot* of people dead. And it left *a lot* of grief stricken families and friends trying to figure out how life was turned upside down on a sunny Tuesday morning. And it left *a lot* of co-workers and survivors fighting to get through the days without harrowing memories and the nights without horrible dreams. And it left *a lot* of citizens attempting to resume a "normal" life in the face of unsettling headlines. I don't know what *a lot* adds up to—I'm not sure anyone will ever be able to calculate them. CNN has not reported the latest count of aching hearts, nervous mothers, weary public servants, or frightened travelers. I just know it's *a lot*.

Upon landing, Frank and I took a cab to the city, checked into our room, and went right back out to catch a cab. We headed toward "Ground Zero." We were left at the curb in front of Trinity Church, which was temporarily closed due to residue. For three blocks, we passed chain link fences stuffed with flowers and photos. Quiet onlookers whispered and snapped photographs. There wasn't much to see. We kept walking.

If the towers were the center of a clock face, then the church was at 6:00. As we approached 8:00, there were many signs warning people not to take photos or video. At 10:00, the street was ripped up, and the usually flat sidewalks were uneven. Exhausted crews covered in sweat and soot dug mechanically while avoiding electrical wires and water lines. At 12:00, we found ourselves walking along the Battery Park City promenade with an inspiring view of Lady Liberty. The late afternoon sun sparkled over the Hudson and for a moment, I reminisced about our best memories of the Big Apple. At the 1:00 mark, we came upon an inlet, which was part of the Manhattan Yacht Club.

We departed the promenade and followed a path into a small park where we found a makeshift memorial. Many hundreds of teddy bears were piled deep and wide along the horseshoe-shaped alcove. Laminated photos, letters, and funeral service programs were pinned to each bear. Flowers were everywhere. There were not too many onlookers. It seemed to be a private, almost sacred place. Perhaps this is where family members were invited to leave something behind. Just as one is compelled to read the names along the Vietnam "Wall" Memorial, so it was natural to read these letters, to glance at photos, to notice dates of birth. All dates of death were the same: September 11, 2001.

I was stunned to see that so many victims were born after 1970. The photos made everything so palpable. Brides, grooms, athletes, graduates, those in uniform, and the families left behind. So many people from so many families—so many names! I came upon an enlarged photo of a beautiful extended family all around the Christmas tree. From the letter attached, I learned that the man who was killed was the proud patriarch standing in the middle of the group portrait.

> *Dear Dad,*
>
> *We miss you terribly and not a day goes by that we don't ache. Your kindness has been a gift to all who knew you and we can't believe your electric smile won't be around to light up the room this Christmas. The twins ask for Pop-Pop every day and we tell them you went on a trip to heaven. Mom hasn't been the same but we promise we'll take good care of her for you. When the time is right, we will all be together again. That will be an amazing reunion. Thanks for being the world's best Dad. You always taught us the importance of honoring God and family. You have given us a good name and we promise to make you proud.*
>
> *Love you forever, Susan*

With swollen eyes, my arm tight around Frank's waist, we walked another two hundred yards to the 3:00 position and found ourselves just one block from the base of the towers. Nothing impeded our view of the charred remains and the heavy equipment. The site was still smoldering. The vivid devastation took on a whole new dimension. It was a horrible sight. *How could this happen in New York?* I wondered. So many names … *Never forget!*

That evening Frank and I attended a dinner function, but because of our individual responsibilities we parted ways the next morning. Outside the hotel door, we hugged longer and harder than usual. He took a taxi to The Bowery to visit a program that mentors youths at risk, and I boarded the Long Island Railroad to speak at a weekend retreat on Long Island. My mind went wandering back to the teddy bears. I kept thinking about the family photo with the touching words written to a beloved father: *"You have given us a good name and we promise to make you proud."*

A good name. A legend is told of a teenage boy in the army of Alexander the Great who ran away from the battle line. He was summoned and when the fearless conqueror learned the boy's name was Alexander, he became even more infuriated. At the mother's pleading and wailing, he spared the boy's life but left him with a final ultimatum; *"Change your ways or change your name!"*

As Christians, we are members of a great family spread across the planet and steeped in a rich two thousand year history. We have the same Savior and we share His good name. I am saddened that I do not always live up to the name "Christian." I am disappointed for not always making choices that would cause my heavenly Father to be proud. I don't want to take the family name lightly. I don't wish to bring shame or rebuke upon it. When I fail to reflect the character of Jesus, I cringe at the thought of God warning me to change my ways or change my name.

Father, you have given me a good name and I promise to make you proud.

I f my people, who are ***called by my name,*** will humble themselves and pray and seek my face and turn from their wicked ways, then I will hear from heaven and will forgive their sin and will heal their land.
—2 Chronicles 7:14

4

How Much Is that Doggy in the Window?

I suppose the self-doubt and second guessing began around the time that the Christian website **Crosswalk.com** started posting chapters from my book on their "Women's Channel." One particular week, they highlighted my essay titled "Dog Dodging." In case you are one of the many millions of Americans who have not read my first book (*Slices of Life*), allow me to provide some helpful context. In short, when she was 5 years old my daughter Paris asked for a puppy. I abruptly said no and thoughtlessly told her she could get one when she turned 10. I never thought she would expect delivery. When she turned 10, I profusely apologized for making a promise I was unable and unwilling to keep. Hence, I received numerous e-mails from across the country:

> *Please let the kids have a dog.*
> *You are depriving your children.*
> *Please tell me the story ends with a new dog.*
> *Get over yourself!*
> *You obviously need counseling.*
>   … and so on …

Only one kind soul wrote to assure me that she knew exactly how I felt about living with animals, and that I wasn't mean or crazy and that, all things considered, I was making the right decision. (It was my mother.) I'm as fragile as the next kid, and those e-mails certainly hurt—and helped.

Was I being narrow minded and self-centered? Would the children develop "issues?" Had I forfeited the joy of putting others before myself? Could I have missed the forest for the trees? Had I overreacted to genuine heartfelt concerns regarding fleas, ticks, drool, shedding, barking, walking, grooming, bathing, teething, and intestinal worms???

Capri (my other daughter) has a good friend named Lara who was her very first playmate when we moved to Reston, Virginia, in 1994. The girls are in the same class at the local public school, they attended the same Christian preschool, and they attend AWANA together each Wednesday night. Lara's mom Monica is an active member of my weekly Bible study.

Monica called one afternoon. She informed me she was about to surprise Lara for her tenth birthday with an adorable Silky Terrier from the local pet store. She quickly inserted an apology for abandoning ship. Until that call, she too, had been an enlightened voice concerning the many valid reasons for NOT owning a pet. I objected, I pleaded, I bargained, I threatened, but alas, it was too late.

Lara told Capri about the joy of owning "Roxy" all during the next school day, and her effusive glee spilled over into late afternoon and early evening phone calls. Lara was obviously the happiest girl in the world. Within 48 hours, Capri became the saddest.

How could I present Capri with a puppy for her tenth birthday when I had denied Paris' requests? (Paris was now nearly 15.) Frank became Swiss and remained neutral on the subject. Up until this episode, he always told the children he had a dog as a boy and would love to own one again. He insisted I was the only one keeping their dream from coming true. Jordan sadly relayed that every candle he ever blew out and every coin he ever tossed into a fountain were accompanied by a single wish that was never fulfilled Ughhh. What would Dr. Dobson do?

The following day, after school, we went to the pet store to visit three very adorable (I must concur) Silky Terrier puppies. They were the siblings of Roxy, who was purchased by my former friend

Monica. The tiniest one was a female weighing in at two and one half pounds. Capri's heart melted, Paris hugged me without being coerced, and Jordan promised to accomplish all kinds of impressive household chores from now until I die. They each offered to pay for their own college tuitions and to give me their firstborn.

We got back in the Durango without a new puppy, and I explained why I did not feel it was a good idea to own a dog at this time in our very busy lives. Besides, everyone tells me that I would be the primary caretaker since I am "around" all day. We drove home in complete silence. Emotionally drained, I got teary at the dinner table. Capri followed. Paris stared blankly. Jordan debated like a trial lawyer. Frank remained in Switzerland, bless his heart. I didn't sleep well that night.

The next morning—in Bible study—I lectured on Colossians 3, in which the apostle Paul exhorts all believers to "put on the new self."

> For you have died, and your life is hidden in Christ.
> Put on a heart of compassion, kindness, humility, gentleness, patience, bearing with one another (and with puppies), forgiveness, and love, which is the perfect bond of unity.
> Let the peace of Christ rule in your heart.
> Whatever you do, do it in the name of the Lord.
> Wives, be submissive to your husbands.
> Husbands, get out of Switzerland (paraphrased).
> Do not exasperate your children, that they may not lose heart.
> Whatever you do, do it for the Lord.
> It is the Lord Jesus Christ whom you serve.

One of the women from the study invited me home for lunch. She "felt moved" to tell me all that God was doing in her life, and she also managed to explain how deprived she felt because her mother would not allow her to have a dog. Her adorable dog sat happily at her feet as she expounded upon the benefits of dog ownership. She showed me his cage, his bed, his leash, his bowls, his toys, and his food. Was it God? Or had my children arranged this?

Whatever it was, I drove directly to PetsMart and proceeded to buy everything my neighbor showed me. I got the right stuff, now all I needed was the dog. I charged the battery for the video camera, called Frank at work, and told him to be home at 6 sharp with the "package."

I was preparing dinner, and the three kids were spread all over the kitchen table and floor doing homework. The garage door went up, Frank walked in with the "package," the video camera clicked on, and the rest is history. After the initial shock, they jumped up and down, and then they started hugging and kissing and thanking Frank. Why were they thanking Frank???

For the first few weeks, when the children put little "Bella" to bed (in the mudroom, of course), she yelped like a coyote under a full moon. She occasionally leaves little deposits around the house. She does not respond to any commands, and she chews on all forms of matter—including Christmas tree ornaments, floor molding, and shoes. Well, at least she's cute.

I can do everything through him who gives me strength. Yet it was good of you to share in my troubles.

—Philippians 4:13-14

5

A Bad Hair Day

I don't know what I was thinking, but then again, that's a fairly common occurrence in my forty-fifth year on the planet. I suppose I was thinking that it would all go smoothly—that I wouldn't run into anyone I know—that I could make it back in fifteen minutes. Wrong, wrong, wrong ... on *all* three counts.

It didn't go smoothly at all, I ran into two people who knew me, and it took thirty-five minutes to get back into the chair at the salon where I was having my hair done. Having one's "hair done" means so many things these days. Not too long ago, it entailed a wash, a trim, and a boofing up. Now, the "menu" is extensive and the prices are expensive. Hair is serious business, and if you don't know exactly what you want, they'll happily serve you extra "portions." Last month, my hip, young Moroccan stylist (I've left the Kuwaiti guy for her) suggested I get a few highlights to "brighten" my dark, one-dimensional drab crown. I assumed she would use a medium brown, but one should never assume. I would say it was more of a burnt orange, autumn, fiery, Ragu red. Maybe I am bonding with the blonde women after all!

When I plunked myself into Najiba's chair that day, I was very clear about what I wanted to order from the menu. A touch up for the gray roots. (Oh, don't we all?) A good cut for the summer heat. The removal of the perpetual flame atop my head. No highlights, thank you, very much. Under protest, she acquiesced.

As usual, the salon was bustling and appointments were running late. Frank was at work, Paris was in Panama for a two-week missions trip, Jordan was at tennis lessons, and Capri was at basketball day camp. By 2:00, I finally got invited to put a robe on. I needed to pick up Jordan by 3:00 sharp and was beginning to feel that clock angst that only a mother can fully understand. The color was applied to my stubborn roots and the rest of my hair was pulled straight up a la Phyllis Diller. I was sent to the hide 'n retreat magazine section of the salon. It began to drizzle, and Jordan called my cell phone. The poor kid was waiting under a tree and informed me lightening had struck. I kicked into Mega Mother Mode and informed Najiba that I had to leave immediately and that I would be back in fifteen minutes. Under protest, she acquiesced.

I noticed the looks on some women's faces as I collected my car keys and cell phone. The receptionist smiled politely as I reached over her counter to whisper "I'll be back." As I sprinted into the rain, I glanced into the shop window to catch a few more looks of disbelief or pity or both.

It was a sunny-turned-rainy July afternoon in beautiful downtown Reston. As I crossed the street toward the parking garage, I heard my name. After three consecutive "ELLIE!"s, I turned around to meet a woman who had recently heard me speak at a luncheon. We ducked under a store awning. She acted as if I looked normal and didn't mention my hair so I *did*. She was animated as she launched into her life story. Apologizing, I explained about Jordan under a tree. She seemed disappointed. I think she was hoping to encounter the woman she had seen speaking from the platform, but was facing instead a frazzled mother in a black nylon robe with hair issues. I wished her well, thanked her for her kind words and asked her to please forget how I looked.

The rain picked up but I didn't mind as it gave me some relief from the burning on my scalp. I made it to the car and gasped at what I saw in the rear view mirror. It was me but by that point looking like Phyllis Diller would have been a big improvement. I was actually more akin to The Creepy Creature from the Black Swamp. The spikes were curling and the color was making its way toward my eyebrows. I grabbed a Kleenex, wiped my forehead, and exited the garage. The tennis courts were only five minutes away and just as I was about to turn into the school, I heard a siren. I did not wait for three sirens.

I pulled over and the officer approached.

"Do you know why I pulled you over?" He looked at my face and then my hair and then he looked away and caught his breath. He stared as a drip of color streamed slowly down my temple, across my left cheek and halted at the corner of my mouth.

"For looking like The Creepy Creature from the Black Swamp?" I arched my eyebrows and cracked a half smile—testing his humor index. He had none.

"Ma'am, you were traveling 34 MPH in a 20 MPH zone."

"But Officer, this road is 35 MPH."

"Not near the school. You should know better."

"I am SO sorry, I thought that sign only applied during September through June."

"Haven't you ever heard of summer school Ma'am?" He wasn't smiling AT ALL.

"Yes, Sir." I explained my predicament and informed him of Jordan's precarious position under the tree and of the imminent danger of him being fried alive and that our precious son is the only one who can carry on the Lofaro family name. I didn't mean to get teary but some color got in my eye (they don't call it chemicals for nothing.) I used some bottled water and found relief—from the eye pain at least. The policeman stood in the rain and watched without emotion. Seemed like a robo-cop, if you ask me.

"License and registration please." I protested (inaudibly) and acquiesced.

He told me to stay in the car. That struck my funny bone and I snickered (audibly) since I hadn't really considered getting out of the car—with the weather—and my hair—and all. He obviously did not own a funny bone. By now, other mothers and babysitters were passing by, slowing down, and cranking their necks to get a closer look at the Swamp Thing. I am sure at least one woman from the PTA Board recognized me.

A full six minutes later, (yes, I counted), he returned with my license and registration, but still no smile.

"Okay, Mrs. Lofaro, consider this a warning. Slow down … and … good luck with your hair." I thanked him profusely and sped into the school parking lot. Jordan was now waiting in a car and I beeped to announce my arrival. There was tapping at my front passenger window. It was Jordan's tennis instructor (whom I had never met) with a big smile and an even bigger umbrella. I slumped in the seat and sheepishly lowered the window. He didn't mention my hair and neither did I. He was a very kind and joyful man.

"You must be Jordan's Mom! I just wanted to let you know that Jordan won a prize for being the most improved player today. He's a terrific young man."

"Thank you. Bye." I pressed the button and the tinted window made him disappear, which is what I wanted to do. Jordan jumped in the car and smirked at me during the five-minute drive back to the salon. I explained that my scalp was burning and that I did not care to discuss the matter until he was in college. The rain stopped, I parked on the street, waved back at a neighbor, and proceeded to have my hair rinsed and cut. I left the salon with rich, deep brown tone on my hair, forehead, and ears.

Talk about your bad hair day! Maybe blonde dye wouldn't have damaged my skin. Maybe gray hair would look more sophisticated. Maybe a crew cut would be carefree. I got home in time to microwave a jar of sauce and boil pasta. To round off the meal, I served Coca-Cola on ice and a steaming hot tube of Pillsbury rolls. My sensitive husband listened to my saga. With one look at the soggy pasta and the yeasty rolls, he insisted we go out to eat. I happily acquiesced.

About the time my natural skin tone returned to various areas of my face, which coincidently was about the same time my roots began to show again, it occurred to me that I had survived my day of humiliation with no lasting scars to my psyche. In fact, God has again reached into the ridiculousness of my daily life to illustrate an important lesson for my soul.

As women, we are bombarded daily with messages about how we need to look, what we need to wear, who we need to be seen with, where we need to live, and so on. The "beauty business" makes billions off our vain pursuits, and most of us regularly contribute to that profit margin. We willingly submit to various forms of torture—trying to perm, pluck, and pierce our way to a standard of beauty determined by somebody else. Why do we do it? Who are we working so hard to please?

It's not that God likes ugly! He just has a different standard of beauty than we are accustomed to. God looks not on the outward appearance, but on the heart (1 Samuel 16:7). "Your beauty should not come from outward adornment, such as braided hair and the wearing of gold jewelry and fine clothes. Instead, it should be that of your inner self, the unfading beauty of a gentle and quiet spirit, which is of great worth in God's sight" (1 Peter 3:3-4).

Now there's a lesson I no doubt will need to learn over and over and over again (but hopefully not in the same, painful way). Maybe God wants me to invest more in activities that develop my *inner* beauty (do you think?).

C harm is deceitful and beauty is passing, but a woman who fears the LORD, she shall be praised.
—Proverbs 31:30 (NKJV)

6

A Hero, a Villain, and God

T hese are two very different stories about two very different men. Both men are deceased. Both of their stories are true. No names have been changed.

The turbulent times of World War II produced many heroes. Butch O'Hare was a fighter pilot assigned to an aircraft carrier in the Pacific. After taking off for one mission with his squadron, Butch looked at his fuel gauge and realized that the technician had neglected to top off his fuel tank. Because of this error, he did not have enough fuel to complete his mission and get back to his ship. When his commander was notified of the situation, Butch was ordered to leave formation and return to the fleet.

As Butch was returning to his ship, he spotted a squadron of Japanese fighter planes on their way to attack the American fleet. With all the American fighter planes gone, the fleet of aircraft carriers was almost defenseless. Realizing that there was only a short window of time to distract and divert the enemy, Butch single-handedly dove into the formation of Japanese planes and attacked.

Butch dove at them repeatedly, firing until all his ammunition was gone. Then he tried to use his plane to clip off wings or tails or anything that would make the enemy planes unfit to fly. He was determined to do everything he could to keep them from reaching the American ships.

Finally, what was left of the Japanese squadron took off in another direction. Butch O'Hare and his fighter plane, both seriously damaged, limped back to the carrier for a turbulent landing. At that time, American planes were equipped with cameras to help the military learn more about enemy maneuvers, the terrain, and key locations. Butch told his story to his fellow soldiers, but the true extent of his heroism was uncovered when the film from the camera in his plane was developed and analyzed.

For his unselfish and courageous acts, Butch was recognized as a hero and given one of the nation's highest military honors. Later on, he was further honored when the busiest airport in the country was given his good name—O'Hare Airport in Chicago.

There was another man named Easy Eddie who worked in Chicago for another perhaps more familiar name—a well-known criminal named Al Capone. Al Capone wasn't famous for anything heroic. Actually, he was notorious for the many murders he committed and the wide extent of illegal things he had done.

Easy Eddie was Al Capone's lawyer, and he was very good at what he did. He skillfully used the law to keep Al Capone out of jail. To show his appreciation, Al Capone paid him a hefty salary and gifted him with extravagant benefits like a home that filled an entire Chicago city block. The house had wrought iron fencing and live-in help and all the conveniences of the day.

Easy Eddie had a son. He loved his son deeply and gave him all the best things while he was growing up; clothes, toys, and a good education. And because he genuinely cared for his son, he knew deep in his heart that he should teach him right from wrong. He was painfully aware that the one thing he couldn't give his son was a good name or a good example. These eluded him, but in time, Easy Eddie decided that his son's future and a good name were more important than riches or power.

A short time later, he went to the authorities to make amends. By telling the truth in court against Al Capone, he knew he was forfeiting his life. Nonetheless, Easy Eddie wanted more than anything to be an example and to do the best he could to give his son a good name. He came to terms with the weight of his marred legacy and he testified against Capone. The authorities finally convicted Capone and within the year, Easy Eddie was shot and killed on a lonely street in Chicago. He was survived by his wife and teenage son.

These two stories seem unrelated unless you know that Butch O'Hare was Easy Eddie's son.

Eddie O'Hare loved Butch so much that he laid down his life to offer him hope for the future. That's what Jesus did for you and me. He laid down His life to give us hope for the future. My history, the good and the bad, pales in contrast with the wonderful plans God has in store for me. What a relief. What a joy. What anticipation.

I don't know for certain Eddie O'Hare's spiritual condition when he met his earthly end. Could it be that his change of heart was the result of a personal encounter with the Maker and Lover of his soul? When Eddie repented of his wrongdoing, he had no idea that the name he sought to restore to his son would likewise be restored to himself. Nothing is too difficult for God! He is in the miracle business, and we must never underestimate what He can create, heal, forgive, reconcile, and reconstruct.

What needs to be "made right" in your life this day? Lay the broken pieces down at the foot of the Cross. You will be amazed by what God can accomplish when you surrender your reputation, your resume, and your rights. Jesus promised that when you lose your life for His sake, you will find it.

It's in dying that we live.

It's in giving that we receive.

It's in breaking that we are made whole.

F or if, when we were God's enemies, we were reconciled to him through the death of his Son, how much more, having been reconciled, shall we be saved through his life!

—Romans 5:10

7

Real Dads

I was racing up and down the aisles of Target last week. I generally enjoy shopping there. They always seem to have what I need when I have no time shop. The local town pool was opening the very next day and the kids needed bathing suits. The ones from last year were worn out, stretched out, faded out, and ruled out. Did I mention they were terminally "pilled?"

One suit for Paris, one for Jordan, and one for Capri. One very cool pair of socks for me. One lavender candle for the guest bathroom, and nothing for Frank. Nothing for Frank? Poor Frank! We whipped through the men's section and stopped at a display of various gifts for Father's Day. It was all the predictable stuff, including T-shirts bearing corny or braggadocio messages. Frank refuses to wear those shirts. He is uncomfortable brandishing the number "1" or the letter "S" on his chest, and he dislikes it when people try to read his body. We were about to head to the register when Capri held up a bright blue shirt with black letters.

"Look Mommy, let's get this for Daddy for Father's Day." I glanced over and proceeded to read the bold lettering; *Real Dads Don't Need Instructions*. Thinking I must have read it incorrectly, I read it a second time … carefully … slowly … aloud. *Real-Dads-Don't-Need-Instructions*. I scrunched my face and read it a third time, louder and with an incredulous, inquisitive tone. *Real Dads*

Don't Need Instructions???

"That is the dumbest thing I have ever heard! What a ridiculous shirt. Whoever wrote that is not a father, or doesn't have a clue about fathering. How ludicrous!"

Paris stared at me and backed away a few feet, in case anyone she knew was in earshot.

Capri shrugged and put the shirt back on the rack. Characteristic of his nature, Jordan came closer and tried to comfort me.

"It's O.K. Mom, they probably didn't mean anything by it. It's just a shirt. If you want a shirt with a meaningful message or a scripture verse, you're probably not going to find it at Target." He proceeded to shuffle through cartoon character boxer shorts and Capri flipped through the ties. Paris smirked and returned to my side. "My goodness Mother, there is no reason to get so worked up over things. What is the big deal? It just means that great Dads know what to do and how to do it."

I felt a sermon coming on. I took a deep breath and summoned the other two. By that time, Jordan had picked out Scooby Doo, Bugs Bunny, Wiley Coyote, and Darth Vader. There they were, all plastered on the front fly of each pair of boxer shorts. Capri had chosen three fairly attractive ties, and they all sighed with disappointment as I ordered each item back to their original point of display. I finally had their attention and so I pointed to the rack where the dumb shirt was hanging.

"That shirt is *completely* preposterous. It is opposed to everything we know to be true about fatherhood. The Bible teaches us that God has supplied *specific* instructions for fathers and that these instructions must be read, memorized, and followed if a father plans to be effective in his children's lives; not to mention the lives of his descendants. Nobody is born knowing God's ways. God's ways must be learned, and He is happy to teach His ways to *anyone* with a desire to learn. It is only by seeking that we find and by asking that we receive. Knowledge and expertise don't happen by accident. Bookstores and libraries offer tons of material on fatherhood but the most important parenting manual in the entire world in the Word of God. A man's relationship with his children can only be as healthy and loving as his relationship with God. And *THAT'S* the truth!"

The children all smiled politely, nodded their heads to reassure me they were listening, and sauntered in a single file toward the check out line. I followed along, like a mother hen, grateful to have shared a teachable moment with her three little chicks. The baby chick was still quite concerned about getting something for Daddy, and I reassured her we would find something for the big rooster during the three weeks that remained before Father's Day. After all, we were on a mission to buy bathing suits, *not* presents!

I shared the experience with Frank that night and he laughed—(I'm never quite sure whether it's *with* me or *at* me, but I do enjoy making him laugh). I hugged him good night and thanked him for being a dad who has followed the instructions—God's instructions.

Except for being Attila the Hun about schoolwork and grades, Frank is a wonderful father. Not only does he study the Word to learn the Lord's mandates for fathers, but he is also an avid reader of Christian literature that encourages men to achieve their fullest potential in their personal and professional lives. I am so happy to be married to a seeker of truth, and the effects of Frank's fathering will be felt for generations. I love that!

Frank spent time overseeing Prison Fellowship's initiatives related to "Children, Youth, and Families." The impact of an incarcerated father is tragic. No one in the family (and ultimately in society) is left untouched. The statistics concerning the negative ripple effects are staggering. A teenage boy who was abandoned by his reckless father had this to say about "Real Dads;"

A Real Dad is kind.

A Real Dad is caring.

A Real Dad walks away from fights.

A Real Dad helps his wife.

A Real Dad helps his kids when they're sick.

A Real Dad doesn't run from his problems.

A Real Dad sticks to his word and keeps promises.

A Real Dad is honest.

A Real Dad doesn't break the law.

His wish list is in stark contrast to the words of a grown daughter at her father's funeral service. He was a wonderful

Christian father who made it his goal to attain wisdom and to follow God's instructions. This particular Dad was a great father because of his devotion to the *greatest* Father.

Dad, are you really gone?
I'm certain I was there when you took your last breath. Yet, it seems your life is still speaking so loud and clear.
Are you really gone?
I can see you in all my childhood days, always taking care of us, letting our lives as children be as God intended: carefree, happy, adventurous, joyful.
Are you really gone?
I can see your smile and your fatherly wink. I feel your familiar and vigorous hug. I can see the joy in your face as your grandchildren embrace you. You turn to me without hesitation and say, "You're a good mother, I'm proud of you."
Are you really gone?
I can see you so clearly; a man of God, a devoted father, a loving husband, a church leader, a friend to many. I can hear you say, "It's good to be alive," as you enjoyed the simple pleasures of this life.
Are you really gone?
I can see and feel your Christian influence woven into the decisions of my life, and it is only by your confident example that I can say; you'll never *really* be gone. And now I can hear our Heavenly Father say to you, "Welcome, good and faithful servant, enter into the joy I have prepared for you."

Real Dads ought to read the instructions. Life is precious and much too short to "wing it."

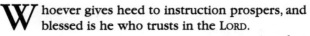

W hoever gives heed to instruction prospers, and blessed is he who trusts in the LORD.
—Proverbs 16:20

8

A Moonlit Memory

In November 2000, I had the privilege of spending a week on "The Women of Faith Caribbean Cruise." My dear friend Kathy Troccoli was the featured singer and was informed she could bring a guest. She invited me. My husband Frank gave his blessing when he learned the cruise was absolutely free and would be attended by 600 women. The long anticipated day finally arrived, and I was thrilled to leave the wintry east coast weather behind—not to mention the laundry, the dishes, and the grocery list.

We set sail on Holland America's *Maasdam* and I immediately adjusted to the good life. The five-course dinners, the island hopping, and the freedom to sleep past the rude awakening of an alarm clock were all delightful treats. To top off the pleasures of cruising, we attended daily gatherings where the Women of Faith worship team ushered us into God's presence and the speakers blessed and challenged us through inspirational talks and Bible study. It was the ultimate retreat.

About the time I was thinking things couldn't get any better, they did! Barbara Johnson, "The Queen of Encouragement," was on board. With over six million books in print, Barbara is considered by many to be the premiere female Christian author in America. Her most popular book to date, *Stick a Geranium in Your Hat and Be Happy*, has sold over one million copies. Imagine my delight when

Barbara Johnson invited Kathy and me to her room for a visit one night after dinner. I happily anticipated how nice it would be to have a personal conversation with a woman whom I had admired for so many years. She had influenced my own speaking and writing style, and I remember feeling a bit like a kid in a candy store. When we arrived at Stateroom 5, Kathy knocked deliberately. What followed still seems a bit dream-like, and a sweet dream at that!

Although Barbara Johnson is known for her zany observations of life, uplifting humor, and cartoonish book covers, in actuality she is a woman well acquainted with grief. Bill and Barbara Johnson gave birth to four healthy boys. One lost his life in the Vietnam War, and another young son was killed by a drunk driver. In the midst of these losses, her husband was struck by a car on a mountainside while on his way to deliver food for a youth retreat. His injuries left him severely disabled and in need of long-term hospitalization. Confined to a veteran's home and declared legally blind, it wasn't until a year later that Mr. Johnson regained his sight and his full health. (The California medical board declared his recovery "an act of God.")

A third son declared his homosexuality and cut family ties for eleven years. He changed his name and returned all letters from his parents. Devastated by her "deposits in heaven," overwhelmed by the helplessness of her husband, and heartsick over the abrupt "loss" of her wayward son, Barbara considered ending her life by driving off a bridge. In one of her early books, *Where Does A Mother Go To Resign?* Barbara bares her soul and shares the dark days that plagued and shook her faith. She tells of how a living, loving God met her on a bridge that tortured day. He literally lifted her unbearable grief and filled her with joy unspeakable. That joy is the trademark of Barbara's ministry to millions.

When Barbara answered the stateroom door, she was wearing a full-length silky robe with a purple floral design. Her slippers were shiny pearl and her typically coifed hair had been brushed out. She greeted us with a hug and informed us her roommate, Linda, had gone for a stroll up on deck. Barbara immediately asked us to join her out on her balcony and informed us there was a present waiting. Kathy and I grinned at one another and shrugged.

As we passed through the glass door, the warm air enveloped us and we turned to see what our hostess had in mind. She pointed toward the full moon. Then holding out her husband's high-powered binoculars, she invited us to enjoy "the gift of the moon in all its glory." Kathy focused in first and then I did the same. Barbara stood between us as we all leaned our forearms on the rail. The ship was moving swiftly and the moon seemed close enough to touch. As the three of us gazed out across those Caribbean waters, Barbara proceeded to eloquently recite a beautiful old hymn, which reminds us that even if all the oceans in the world were ink, it would not be enough to write of God's goodness and mercy. I realized at that point that this was one of those "moments" that would leave a deep imprint on my heart.

We moved back into the cabin and sat in a cozy living room. The glass door to the balcony was left open and the sounds of the ship cutting through the sea provided a soothing backdrop to our conversation. Barbara asked about us. She took a sincere interest in my new book and Kathy's new role as a keynote speaker. When we attempted to be inquisitive about her illustrious career, she promptly deflected any kudos. She insisted she was not a great writer and explained that her bestseller was put together by the publisher after they forced her to mail in her speaking tapes. She laughed out loud about being a panelist at an upcoming writer's conference.

Then Barbara leaned forward and talked about heaven. She spoke of the glorious reunion with her two precious sons and she shared that her husband has instructed her not to cancel her appearance at a Women of Faith Conference if he "passes" first. She told us she planned to be gone before long and was quite peaceful about the prospect of "going home." She leaned a bit closer and whispered her belief that if people really understood heaven, they would lose all fear of death.

A hush fell upon the room, and I was reminded of my whereabouts. Kathy and Barbara continued to talk, and my thoughts continued to drift. I had gone on the cruise anticipating the long walks on the beach, the sun drenched days, and the starry nights. I was anxious to catch up on my reading, to nap by the pool, and to lose all sense of time. It would also be a week when I had hoped to encounter the Lord in new ways. I wanted to see Him in all the beauty of my surroundings and feel His presence in the deep rest that awaited me.

Little did I know that my sweetest encounter with Christ on that cruise ship would be through a 73 year old woman who had weathered many storms. It was obvious to me that her loss had produced abundance. Her pain had resulted in compassion. Her desperate need to make sense of death led her to the cross—and there she found a resurrected life. She has gracefully poured out her joyful and compassionate life, and on that remarkable moonlit night I was so happy to soak it in. I had spent an evening with a friend of God.

Postscript: Several months after the cruise, Barbara was diagnosed with a brain tumor. Surgery and chemotherapy and radiation and countless medications all followed. Almost two years have passed and she is still facing each day as a warrior. In the midst of her fiercest battle, she has blessed us with yet another book, *Stick a Geranium in Your Cranium.* Barbara Johnson has chosen to bring hope and healing to others in the midst of her own pain and suffering. She has chosen to use a hospital bed as a platform. She has chosen to continue to focus on other people's hurts instead of her own. Barbara Johnson has chosen life. Fruitful ... abundant ... eternal.

Y ou have made known to me the path of life; you will fill me with joy in your presence, with eternal pleasures at your right hand.

—Psalm 16:11

9

Cold Cut Love

The Reverend Billy Graham's lovely wife Ruth once said; "I don't believe in divorce—but I have considered murder." I've always liked that woman. I'm sure Ruthie and I would get along quite well. Of course I have no intention of ever bringing harm to Frank, but to deny fleeting feelings of aggression would be ingenuine. Allow me to share the story of the smoked turkey. (Well, it actually goes much deeper than the smoked turkey, but you already knew that.)

After 20 years of marriage, I thought it would be safe to assume certain things. A reasonable person should be aware of the likes and dislikes of her spouse. A reasonable person should have some idea of what kind of gift his mate would enjoy or where she would like to spend a vacation. A reasonable person should be able to expect his or her mate to bring home an entertaining video from Blockbuster. A reasonable person should know his mate's opinion of wasabi, lentils, goat cheese, curried chicken, root beer, and smoked turkey. Well ... Frank has been unreasonable.

My husband works a half-day on most Saturdays. He says it keeps him ahead of the curve. He says it makes him more confident on Monday mornings. He says he needs to be a good example to the others. I say he's escaping Saturday morning chores around the house and that he loves breakfast at the diner, the morning paper and Starbucks. I let it go—because I'm reasonable.

My husband's favorite comedy is "It's a Mad, Mad, Mad, Mad World" and his favorite drama is "Twelve Angry Men." Whenever he stops to rent a movie, he usually brings home one or the other. When he's in the mood for high adventure, he shows up with "The Great Escape." I used to enjoy those three films, but now I dislike them. (The children have memorized the scripts.) I smile and watch—because I'm reasonable.

My husband gave me "sleepwear" for my last birthday. Of course, nobody could actually sleep in the item he bought because it would give any woman a royal wedgie. I held it up to the light three different ways to figure out where the escape hatch was, but to no avail. I wore it (okay—only once) because I'm reasonable. Now let's move on to the smoked turkey saga.

My husband occasionally brings home cold cuts and rolls on Saturday afternoons. Of course, that's a kind effort and we deeply appreciate the gesture. He has known me more than twenty years and he has known the children all their lives. The children and I abhor smoked turkey. It's usually pinkish and tastes more like very salty ham. We find the smoked taste quite despicable. On the other hand, we love the roasted homestyle turkey which they will gladly slice (any thickness one desires) at our local supermarket. It is quite delicious, always fresh, never salty and by gosh—it tastes just like turkey. For variety, we enjoy roast beef, ham, and Swiss cheese. Whenever Frank arrives with smoked turkey (always a pound of it), he also brings American salami that tastes just like hot dogs (always a pound of it). We do not enjoy either of those items. Never have—never will. However, we say grace, spread a half a cup of mayo on the roll and eat what's in front of us—because we're reasonable.

I've talked to Frank numerous times about the family's food preferences, with extra emphasis on my own particular tastes. One Saturday, Frank arrived home from his half day of work at 2:15. We expected him by 12:30 but he called at 1:45 to say he was running late. He said he had just pulled into the supermarket and I gently reminded him that we prefer the *homestyle* turkey, rolls *without* seeds, *non*-sour pickles, and *plain* potato chips. I believe his parting words were "Got it."

We finally sat down to a late lunch at 2:30. I set the table and put out the condiments and we bowed our heads for grace. By the time our youngest child completed her prayer, I lifted my head to see Frank stuffing things into the kitchen garbage bin.

"What are you doing?" I asked him.

"Getting a head start."

"On what?"

"Cleaning up!"

"Frank, please sit down." The turkey was passed (along with a pound of the weird salami). It looked a kind of pink but Frank suggested it was probably a bit undercooked. I assembled my long anticipated sandwich and took a big bite while the kids chatted about their week at vacation bible school. I chatted and chewed and then my mouth froze.

"Is this *smoked* turkey?"

"Nope."

"It *tastes* like smoked turkey."

"Well, it's not."

"Frank, are you sure?"

"Yep."

"Did you specifically *ask* for the homestyle turkey?"

"I pointed at it through the glass—it's homestyle."

"Did you ever *mention* "homestyle?"

"Ellie, I told you I pointed at it."

"*This* is smoked turkey."

"But I didn't *ask* for smoked turkey."

"But you didn't *ask* for homestyle either!"

"It's fine—*just eat it.*" I believe that was the wrong thing for him to say at that particular moment. Never mind that the pickles were sour. Never mind that he brought home a two-liter bottle of root beer. Never mind that the rolls had garlic flavoring. My blood pressure and voice rose simultaneously. I no longer felt the desire to be reasonable.

"Whaddya mean 'Just eat it'—why do we have to eat smoked turkey when we *hate* smoked turkey???" Frank responded with a passive-aggressive-quasi-spiritual-reverse-psychological comment in a calm, monotonal voice and once again, I looked like the one with the problem. I shot back one more objection and proceeded to eat my smoked turkey on a garlic roll (with a grateful heart, of course, due to Frank's timely statistics concerning the population of the world facing daily hunger.) UGHHH!

The lunch "God provided" was eaten, the kids scrambled in three directions and Frank grabbed the paper and went for a nap. I cleared and rinsed and wiped and lifted the garbage bin to discard the paper plates. There they were; the wrapping of the cold cuts with the price tags and labels affixed. The first crunched bag: "Hard Salami." — the second: "Smoked Turkey." I descended the basement steps, bags in hand. Frank pretended to be asleep. I got close to his face.

"You lied about the smoked turkey and then you tried to hide the evidence!"

"I pointed to the homestyle turkey, the lady made a mistake."

"But you *saw* the label."

"Only after I got home, and I knew you'd be mad so I did what I had to."

"Did you think I would be fooled? Did you think you'd get away with it?"

"Okay, you caught me. Call the turkey police." He rolled over.

"Is that it? Are we done? Aren't you even going to apologize?"

"I apologize. Next time I'll buy homestyle turkey because making you happy is my goal. It's what I live for. Can you scratch my back?"

Completely unreasable.

B ear with each other and forgive whatever griev-
ances you may have against one another. Forgive
as the Lord forgave you.

—Colossians 3:13

10

My White House Moment

My office phone rang and, as usual, I let the answering machine answer it (isn't that what it was made for)? There was a smart, youthful, chipper voice on the other end. I can tell you what she said—verbatim—because I have saved her message and I played it back several times; twice for myself, once for Frank, and once for the kids.

Hi Mrs. Lofaro, this is Lindsay Limeater calling from the White House Social Office. On behalf of the President, I am calling to invite you to a reception for the National Day of Prayer. Refreshments will be served in the State Dining Room and the Ceremony will follow in the East Wing Ballroom. It will be held on Thursday, May 2. You will be one of two hundred special guests and you'll need to come to the East Visitor's Gate at 2:30 pm. You will need to have your photo ID. You will need to be in business attire and due to security purposes, we ask that you do not bring any gifts for the President. Please let us know if you are able to attend. When you call, we will need to verify your Social Security number, and we will be glad to answer any questions. We hope to see you there.

I was quite pleased and impressed and thrilled and I waited

for dinnertime to make my grand announcement.

"You'll *never* guess where I have been invited!" My nose was pointed a bit skyward. The four of them were unmoved except when they reached for the serving bowls. Sweet Jordan decided to make an effort.

"Another speaking engagement, Mom?"

"Nope!"

Paris wryly took another stab.

"To be a guest on a new version of 'Survivor'?"

"Nope!"

Capri looked hopeful. "To work in the cafeteria again?"

"No baby girl—I did that already. The Lord has delivered me from that place."

Frank couldn't constrain himself.

"To show women how laundry can get done without sorting or ironing?"

"Not funny, honey. No, no, no to *all* your guesses! Okay, are you ready? I AM GOING TO THE WHITE HOUSE!!! The White House! Can you believe it? Isn't that an honor? Isn't that exciting?" Frank asked if he was invited.

"No, because you are not grateful for clean laundry."

"How would the White House know that?"

"Highly sophisticated intelligence—they know a lot."

"Why would they invite YOU to the White House?"

"I don't know. I thought YOU would know! Do you think Chuck and Patty (Colson) got me on the list?"

"No. Not without putting me on it too. Do you think it's your new book?"

"No way. Only five thousand copies were sold so far. Not exactly the big time."

"Frank, it's probably that guy you know who works for the new Faith Based Initiative. He really likes you. Maybe they needed more women in the room."

"Maybe. But I doubt it. Maybe they want you to run in 2008."

"Right."

I cleaned the kitchen and ran down the basement stairs to the phone machine. I invited the kids to join me and they did. Frank went to the bathroom instead. I played the message and received a couple of smiles, a pat on the back, a high five, and one "That's cool, Mom." They scattered to do their homework and I played the message again as I leaned back in my desk chair. This time, I started letting my mind wander and wonder.

One of two hundred special guests? Photo ID? Social Security? Business attire? No gifts? (Too bad—I thought I might offer Frank. He's so full of solutions). Why was I invited? Who else will be there? Will I meet George? Do women still curtsy? Should I buy a new girdle? Are cameras allowed? Have we paid all our taxes?

The National Day of Prayer came quickly and I found myself excitedly entering the East Gate. I passed through the surveillance cameras and the scanners and the under wire in my bra set off the metal detectors. Two Secret Service men rushed in to frisk me and I informed them of my support system. They nodded politely and backed away. Marines in full regalia directed us through a long corridor and up the grand staircase. The upper foyer housed wonderful portraits, magnificent tapestries, and more Marines. This time, they were performing in an ensemble. I proceeded to the State Dining Room and was amazed by the size of the oval table. One could not help but wonder how many thousands of interesting people have dined there in the past two hundred years. I milled around the room and tried not to stare at anybody. It was difficult.

I picked up a beverage and proceeded to "scope" the room. Chuck and Patty Colson were there. What a privilege it has been to have co-labored with them for eight years. Their devotion to the high calling of ministering to "the least of these" has impacted our lives dramatically. Shirley Dobson was there. She has been Chairperson of The National Day of Prayer since 1988. Her husband Jim was along for support. Vonette Bright was also there. Her husband Bill had been struggling with illness so she graciously attended as the ambassador of Campus Crusade for Christ. What an incredible impact their labor of love has had on every continent of the planet. My favorite talk show host, Janet Parshall was there. (Someday, I hope to have her vocabulary.) The esteemed Dr. Lloyd Ogilvie, Chaplain of the U.S.

Senate, was there. So was the great thinker Dr. Ravi Zacharias, and the President of Moody, Dr. Joseph Stowell. I behaved well and didn't take any pictures and didn't violate anybody's personal space—unless they smiled at me.

At 3:30, we were all invited to proceed down the corridor, along the red carpet, and into the East Wing Ballroom. The huge double doors were wide open, and the room was bright yellow with dazzling chandeliers. A podium bearing the Presidential Seal stood atop a small platform straight ahead in the center, and chairs were arranged on each side of the aisle. Along the back and side walls, photographers and cameramen hovered atop narrow risers. They were all wearing those nifty vests with lots of pockets.

Secret Service Agents were posted at the four corners of the room and the bright camera lights were glaring. Finally the people were settled and there wasn't a bad seat in the house that day. My heart raced a bit. The Dobsons entered with Dr. Ogilvie and a fabulous African American Choir sang a hymn. Then a commanding, but invisible voice came over the PA system.

"Ladies and Gentleman, The President and Mrs. Laura Bush." I jumped to my feet and a guy in front of me started clicking away with his camera. Nobody stopped him, so I did what every red blooded American would do. I started clicking away too. I got three great shots and my battery went dead. Mrs. Dobson made opening remarks and the Senate Chaplain prayed in his soothing baritone voice before he welcomed Mrs. Bush to the podium. She read from Psalm 91 and commented briefly on what it has meant to her in such a trying year. She then spoke the following words, *"I am so grateful to be married to a man who is strong enough to take on the problems of the world and humble enough to go the Lord for help and guidance."*

When she introduced the President, he emerged from his seat, got to the podium, told us that he loves being Laura Bush's husband and proceeded to kiss her gingerly. She was beautiful and he was handsome and they poignantly expressed their love for God and for one another and for their country.

I was fully alive to every dimension of the moment, and I was thrilled to witness just a small slice of our great history. I felt proud to be an American and grateful to have a leader who knows where his help comes from. God bless our President. God bless our leaders—federal, state, and local. God bless our military. And God bless America ... land that I *deeply* love.

We wait in hope for the LORD; he is our help and our shield. In him our hearts rejoice, for we trust in his holy name. May your unfailing love rest upon us, O LORD, even as we put our hope in you.
—Psalm 33:20-22

11

"Hello Mudduh ...
Hello Fadduh ... "

Kamp Kanakuk is considered by many to be the best Christian camp in the country. Thousands of kids have passed through there every summer since 1925, so there is quite an extensive alumni list. It's a high energy, high adventure, high profile kind of place. The director of the camp, Dr. Joe White, has written a book called *Life Training,* and that's exactly what goes on at Kanakuk. Frank and I heard so many rave reviews, we finally looked into it. Great website, great facilities, great staff, great reputation. Even Max Lucado wrote very lovingly about Kamp Kanakuk.

On July 21st, we put Paris and Jordan on a plane to Branson, Missouri, for what we hoped would be the greatest adventure of their lives. They were so excited as they boarded the plane, and Capri was equally excited about being an only child for two whole weeks. Hugs and kisses and reminders and warnings and promises and they were off. Frank couldn't believe I cried. *Men ...*

That was a Saturday. Weeks earlier, we were assigned a Username and a Password to enter the "Parents Place" once we visited their website. I assumed (you know what happens when you assume), that if *we* had e-mail access, that the *kids* would have e-mail access. Wrong. I assumed they could e-mail us daily since phone calls were not allowed. Wrong. I assumed I would hear from my little petunias during the first few days. Wrong. They left Saturday at noon and arrived at the camp Saturday night. After nearly four days without kid contact, I was not pleased. On Wednesday, I started my e-mail campaign to various "officials" at Kamp Kanakuk:

Dear So and So,

Could you please check to see if Paris and Jordan Lofaro are alive? I would greatly appreciate your immediate response. And could you please move more quickly than the Missouri mail? It seems very odd to me that the campers cannot return e-mail. I really think you should change that policy. Makes no sense.

In Jesus' love,
Ellie Lofaro

I shot this off to three or four people who were "in charge," according to the website. Of course, I did not bother Dr. White—I *know* my bounds.

They all responded by the next morning, bless their hearts. Paris and Jordan were doing just fine and one of them even reported having spotted Paris "smiling big." I felt some small comfort (very small) but that afternoon, I ran to the mailbox at the first sound of the mail truck brakes. Capri followed close behind—it felt like a scene from an old war movie. There were three letters for me and Frank and two for Capri. Jackpot! I ripped mine open as if my next breath was to be found inside. I read Jordan's letter first:

Dear Mom and Dad,

Camp is great! We had church this morning in the woods and the speaker really made me think about God. We have a lot of fun activities and I'm learning a lot. The main thing I have learned is that I should always be third. (Jesus first, others second). I signed up for football and I made a lot of friends. They also have a lot of water sports at the lake, paintball, archery and other stuff. My cabin is great and

the food is great. During free time, I am keeping up
with my Bible reading. I really feel that I have gotten
closer to God. I miss you guys soooo much. I think
about you every day. I'll tell you all the details when
I get home. Sorry Mom, I am not keeping a journal.
Our cabin is awesome. I have to go now. I love you.
Thanks for sending me here.
     Bye. Jordan
     P.S. I definitely want to come back next year !!!

It was Jordan's first and last letter from Kamp Kanakuk. He was obviously a very fulfilled young man. On the other hand, Paris wrote once or twice *each* day. Her letters suggested that she was *not* a happy camper:

Dear Mom and Dad,
     I miss you so much it's not even funny! It's so
hot here and I can't get clean. I have HAD IT with
insects. If I ever become President, I will make them
illegal. I am so sick of taking a shower only to get
sweaty again! I took the ropes course and got five big
bug bites and a rope burn on my neck. I had fun
kayaking yesterday but I hated the dance class.
Tubing was good. It rained very heavily today—a glo-
rious downpour. There was a sudden thunderstorm
in the middle of the Bible study, and I prayed really
hard that it would be really serious so we would all
have to be evacuated. I lost a sock and a white towel
and I was starting to grow a unibrow, but fortunate-
ly, I found my tweezers. I saw Jordan. He seems pretty
happy. I miss everyone soooo much and I can't wait
to come home! Is there any way I can leave sooner?
Please???

To make sure we had not missed one drop of her pathos, she had thoughtfully included a simple list enti-tled *The Top Ten Things I Miss:*

1. Capri
2. Mom and Dad
3. feeling clean
4. air conditioning
5. Sprite
6. my CD player
7. television
8. movies
9. clean clothes
10. a bug free environment

I'm out of stamps, paper and envelopes. Write soon and send some. I've been reading my Bible, but I haven't memorized any verses because it's too hot.

Love and hugs and kisses,

Your dear but sweaty daughter Paris

P.S. Only eleven days left to go!!!

I laughed as I read those letters and I cried and I marveled at how kids who are growing up under the same roof can be so different. I shook my head in amazement.

I wonder if God shakes His head at me some days. He sent me here on a most exciting adventure, and I often make lists of what I'm forced to deal with and what I don't have. How grateful I have become for His mercy and grace. How I yearn to experience joy in *every* circumstance. How I covet the wisdom and understanding to count all things loss for the sake of the Gospel. I meditated a long while on the camp motto: "I'm Third."

Not quite yet, but I'm working on it, Lord.

F or by the grace given me I say to every one of you: Do not think of yourself more highly than you ought, but rather think of yourself with sober judgment, in accordance with the measure of faith God has given you.

—Romans 12:3

12

The Prodigal Father

prodigal *(prod i gal), adj. 1. wastefully or recklessly extravagant; 2. giving profusely; 3. lavishly abundant.*
n. 4. a person who spends money or uses resources with wasteful extravagance.[1]

A re you surprised by Mr. Webster's definition of prodigal? I was. There was a time when I thought it meant disobedient. Then I decided it meant repentant. I never had cause to "look the word up" being that neither my public school nor my catechism classes ever touched upon the story of that infamous bad boy. When I learned the proper definition of the word prodigal, the story from Luke 15 certainly took on a whole new meaning (no pun intended).

There are three very different and very intriguing characters in this parable from Jesus. The plot has subplots, it's both painful and hopeful, and it has a happy ending. It covers themes such as free will, the desire of the flesh, the draw of the world, rightful inheritance, poverty, sibling rivalry, jealousy, forgiveness, humility, generosity, mercy, and that's just the beginning!

My prodigal father wasn't born into a family of any particular social standing. His parents were immigrants from the south of Italy. They were prototypes of the hundreds of thousands who poured into Ellis Island after the turn of the century. My paternal grandmother (who I am named for) was married by the age of 15. She had 13 pregnancies, 12 deliveries, and raised 11 children in a brownstone on Herkimer Street in Brooklyn. I was 9 when she died, but I remember her very well. She was a heavy-set woman with a bun atop her thick white hair, a gold tooth, a mole, an apron (I think it was permanently attached), and soft hands that seemed to glisten from such frequent contact with olive oil. Back in those days, everyone worked and everyone handed their earnings over to the head of the household—for which they received the company of each other and 3 meals a day.

When my Dad (number 9 of the 11) was stationed in Tripoli, Libya, he met my Mom and later returned there as a civilian to marry her. She went from hanging out at the beach under the palm trees to hanging out at the brownstone under the clothesline. I was born there. Insurance courses and night shifts that followed day shifts resulted in financial blessing which resulted in financial burden (i.e., the more you have the more you need).

Dad was in pursuit of the American dream, and I guess he woke up one day to find that his dream was reality. Bigger houses, bigger cars, bigger pool. More clothes, more restaurants, more landscaping. Nobody was complaining. It was a great time to be a kid.

What we didn't realize then was the enormous pressure my father was under to keep his dream afloat. He was raised in the old school where men don't share their feelings of fear, frustration, or failure. Dad came from simple means, and his achievements meant a great deal to him. His siblings always dropped over with friends to show off their brother Al's place. Look at Al's wooded acre. Look at Al's grand colonial. Look at Al's yard.

But nobody was really looking at Al. His self-esteem became quite interwoven with his worldly possessions, so when Black Tuesday hit the American economy in 1979, my father did what most American did not do. He kept spending. He kept up with the Joneses. He kept up appearances. Sadly, he woke up one day to find his dream had become a nightmare. Debt had mounted, his insurance agency had problems, and his wife of 25 years had filed for divorce. The house was sold as was the agency which bore his name. Their marriage ended one year later.

Fast forward 22 years. Dad lives in a small condo in south Florida. He is a gourmet cook, an accomplished oil painter, a ballroom dancer, and an exercise enthusiast. He rides his bicycle a few miles each day, and swims 50 laps in the local pool. This discipline has been a response to diabetes and a quadruple bypass he underwent 10 years ago. He watches his weight, keeps a year round tan, and looks pretty healthy at 72. Imagine my shock when his sister Ida (who lives next door to him) called me crying. She is 85, fully operative, and more "colorful" than ever. She is prone to dramatics so I responded calmly.

"Hi Aunt I, what's up in sunny Florida?"

"Never mind the weather! Your father's dying!"

"How do you know?"

"He looks terrible and he's always tired and he's been mean to me."

"I'm sorry Aunt Ida. I think sometimes he takes you for granted."

"He went for a test and his heart is bad and he doesn't want another operation."

"What's the matter with his heart?"

"He's having a hard time breathing and his valve is no good anymore. You better talk to him 'cause he's not listening to me. That's the thanks I get."

"Is he there?"

"Nope. He's next door sleeping. He's sleeping too much and hasn't gone out and he's in serious trouble and he's so darn stubborn. Maybe he'll listen to you. Call him!"

"Don't worry, I will. Calm down. And you take it easy Aunt I."

I did call and I was taken aback to hear how weak and feeble my father sounded. He was breathing laboriously and was characteristically stubborn as I probed for answers. He did NOT want any of us coming there and he did NOT want surgery and he did NOT want pity! I left him with a prayer and a challenge to take some type of action. Two days later, he admitted himself to the Miami Veteran's Hospital and agreed to open heart surgery. I initiated a few prayer chains and then called family. The phone calls to the hospital room of my independent and sometimes aloof Father began to stream in. His children, his siblings, his ex-wife. Many tender words broke through the dam of hurt, regret, and unkept promises.

My conversation with him the night before the surgery is one I will not forget. It ended with a powerful truth.

"God loves you, Daddy."

"You better believe it."

"I do, Daddy. YOU better believe it."

The next morning, my father was shaved, prepped, and given anesthesia by 7 A.M. The cardiologist ordered one more test. Aunt Ida, Uncle Tony, and Aunt Mary settled into the waiting room for what they thought would be a dreadfully long day. My sister and I decided to fly down in two shifts to nurse him after his week of hospital recovery. I was told not to expect a call until mid to late afternoon, so when the phone rang at 10 A.M., my heart sank. It was Aunt Ida. This time she sounded kind of dazed and disoriented.

"Your father's not going to die."

"What happened?"

"They did another test and his valve is healed."

"Healed? What kind of healed?"

"They said it was working at 30% capacity and now it's over 90%. They cancelled the valve replacement. He's coming home for lunch. He's a lucky dog."

"Lucky dog? Lucky dog nothin'! He's a blessed son of God! He's a miracle! He's going to be a testimony! That's fantastic! Thank you Jesus! God is great!"

I did a little jig. Aunt Ida sounded nonplussed. The Lord had answered my prayer and touched my father's diseased heart. The phone rang again. A dear friend called to say she had prayed that my father would not die before he commits his life—heart, mind, and soul—to Jesus. Lord, hear our prayer.

> God did this so that men would seek him and perhaps reach out for him and find him, though he is not far from each one of us.
>
> —Acts 17:27

13

Never Say Never

Bella Mia Lofaro had quickly turned six months old, and we celebrated the occasion. Her Italian name is quite apropos—it means "My Beauty." She is healthy, she is adorable, she is sweet, and she is our precious baby girl. Never mind that she is a dog. A tiny Silky Terrier, to be exact.

Anyone who knows me casually or intimately is completely incredulous concerning this unforeseen family addition. I have never had a dog. I don't particularly care for dogs. I had no intention of living with a dog. My children clearly understood that they would never experience dog ownership until they moved out. I am a loving and compassionate mother so I did compromise to some extent and allowed guinea pigs and fish into the home. They all died prematurely.

So, what happened? Why the sudden change of heart?

I don't know. I'm still trying to figure that out. I have earnestly attempted to retrace my steps—to review my thoughts—to discover the moment when everything in my neatly tucked away file labeled "DOG" was somehow retrieved, rearranged, and revised. Talk about a paradigm shift!

In my first book, *Slices of Life,* I penned two essays about my aversion toward having a pet. "Dog Dodging" and "Confessions of a (non) Pet-Lover" summed up my sentiments perfectly—"no dog ...

no way … no how." I was resolute. I was steadfast. I was immovable. I was firm.

Well, we've had Bella almost four months now, and I can honestly say it's felt like forever. If I had a life before owning a dog, I don't remember it. The weekdays between April and June dragged on while the kids were at school and Frank was at work. The dog had to be fed and walked and smiled at and held and comforted when she felt lonely. My quiet days of typing and reading and preparing messages for retreats were rudely interrupted. I had died to self but was not experiencing the blessing. It was time for a family meeting.

"I am a very busy woman and I cannot stay at home with 'a baby.' My last baby went off to kindergarten five years ago and I like my 9 to 3 routine. This puppy seems to need a mother and I did not sign up for that!"

I offered to find Bella a better home. (So much for building trust with one's children.) Fortunately, their reaction is not on video. I retracted my comment and we brainstormed and found out that very small dogs can have doggy litters quite similar to kitty litters. I bought two containers and two big bags of whatever that stuff is that very day. One went in the laundry room between the kitchen and the garage, and one went in the basement playroom. The problem was solved. Well, that is, until she pooped. It did not occur to me that a tiny dog could produce such hefty deposits. They looked much smaller outdoors. Nor did it occur to me that our home would soon smell like a stable. Nor did it occur to me that Bella's toilet didn't flush. The garbage can in the kitchen became an environmental hazard. The Department of Health would have not been pleased. It was time for another meeting.

"I cannot live in a zoo, and I cannot have that odor in the kitchen or the playroom or the laundry room. Especially the laundry room! I spend half my life in the laundry room, and that odor is stealing my joy!"

This time, I knew better than to suggest sending Bella to foster care. The children listened carefully and promptly created a new chore chart with more frequent doo-doo patrols. They now remove the radioactive material directly to the garage and they leave the window open a few inches. They signed up for an eight week puppy training class, and we are keeping up with all the necessary veterinarian care. Bella has gotten shots for Distemper, Canine Hepatitis, Leptospirosis, Parainfluenza, Coronavirus (from Queens?), Bordetella (kennel cough), Lyme Disease, and Rabies. She also takes a monthly pill for worms. She's a healthy baby.

One night during the last week of school, Bella tried to climb the gate from the laundry room (where she sleeps) to the kitchen. Her right foot, I mean paw, got caught and she cried in pain. We all raced downstairs and the kids freed her leg and held her close and comforted her. She was limping. It was well past midnight. The vet on call suggested a clinic I was unfamiliar with. It was thirty minutes away. Frank advised that we wait until morning and the children cried and told him it would be his fault if the dog died during the night. Frank held his ground and we all went to bed.

The children went off to school at 6:30, 8, and 9 am respectively. Each one made me pronounce an oath concerning my follow up care of Bella. I made three sincere oaths and when the last bus was boarded, Bella and I headed to the vet. I asked them to do an x-ray. It was 9:30 A.M. and I was informed that Bella would have to spend the day for observation. I kissed her (a first) and handed her over to a stranger (a first) and got in the car and cried for my baby (a first). Maybe I am her mother after all.

Endnote: Bella incurred a minor sprain and is now back to full speed. No one is able to "catch" her and she does not respond to "Come!" It's time for another family meeting.

A bove all, my brothers, do not swear—not by heaven or by earth or by anything else. Let your "Yes" be yes, and your "No," no, or you will be condemned.

—James 5:12

14

It's Better in the Bahamas

I am so busy. There's no time for lunch with *anybody*. (Who *are* those women who "do lunch?") Frank is busy, too. We haven't had a complete conversation in weeks. The kids are also busy. Their recreational, social, and spiritual calendars are booked through next year. I didn't send out Christmas cards in 2001. I had high hopes for 2002. Maybe I'll send the family photo for Valentine's or Easter or for Independence Day. I could do a whole patriotic motif. Busy, busy, busy.

Oops. A friend of mine told me to stop using the word BUSY. She suggests, instead, to say that life is FULL. She has decided that BUSY means Buried Under Satan's Yoke. On the other hand, she says that FULL means Faithful Under the Lord's Leading. She also contends that being BUSY is exhausting and being FULL is exhilarating. Being BUSY is self-directed and being FULL is God-ordered. Sounds terrific, but I wonder if my life would be better characterized as BULL. (Buried Under the Lord's Leading.) After all, I *am* exhausted and I *am* doing my best to serve the kingdom and a few of its inhabitants. Isn't it better to "burn out" for Jesus than to "rust out?" Isn't the harvest full? Aren't the workers few? Don't the days seem shorter? Will the toilets ever clean themselves?

I'm not complaining—and I believe my friend's theory has some merit. When God orders my (full) day, there is peace and fortitude, no matter how many demands are made on my body, mind, and soul. However, I can't agree with the part about exhaustion. I go to bed exhausted at the close of many days when I know that I have served the Lord wholeheartedly. Whether I've been overly busy or full, I realized it was time to get away.

I couldn't remember the last time Frank and I got away together. I mean *really* away and *really* together. On a recent Sunday afternoon, we locked our bedroom door and tried to find some "alone time." One of the kids knocked and we told them to go away. Five minutes later, the phone rang. It was Capri calling us from the second phone line in the basement. "Hi! Whatcha doin'?" Frank explained we were napping and hung up. It was time to run away.

We celebrated our twentieth anniversary on March 7, 2002. Marrying Frank J. Lofaro, Jr. was the second best decision of my life. I would like to figure out where twenty years went. Oh well, that's another story. We couldn't get reasonable airfares because of spring break, and we didn't want to be away from the children for Easter, so we finally took on April 7 to spend three whole days—all alone—on an island—in the Caribbean. From the moment we landed in Freeport on Grand Bahama Island that sunny Sunday afternoon to the time we flew home a few days later, we had a great sense of well-being.

The island is a very peaceful one. The people are full of joy. Even with such a small population, the churches dot the landscape in every direction. Many Bahamians told us that theirs is a "Christian nation." This is not to say that others would feel unwelcome. On the contrary, the love of Christ is evident there and we were continually surprised to observe Jesus Christ being glorified everywhere we went and in every conversation we had with the natives.

It began with the hotel van driver at the airport. Frank customarily hangs back while I enter into conversation with strangers. I leaned forward and smiled, "The weather is beautiful here. We left rain and clouds in Washington D.C."

"Ohhh yes Mam. Da good Lord has blessed us with blue skies and sunshine."

The hotel receptionist referred to the Lord with the same ease and that night, the taxi driver did the same on the short ride to dinner. Frank asked him about the extent of damage from their last hurricane.

"God protected us and He was with us and we praise Him for never abandoning us."

The seafood was fabulous, but somehow, it tasted even better that night. The waiter was so kind and the busboy explained his intentions to make a difference for Jesus by attending seminary. He is working hard and saving money to do so. The next day, we rented a Jeep for a few hours and drove around the island. Imagine my delight when I turned on the radio and heard many familiar Christian singers. On a secular pop station, a commercial came on announcing that Psalty, the Singing Songbook (a Christian ministry to children) would be coming to Grand Bahama. The two shows were sponsored by Kentucky Fried Chicken and McDonalds! (Why can't WE do that???)

We strolled through the International Market on our third and final day on the island. It was an outdoor, colorful place with mostly handcrafted goods. The women who ran the stalls were full of expression and laughter and song, which clearly portrayed a sweet peace and an abiding faith. As usual, "Mr. Bargain-till-they-Bleed" approached the vendors with one agenda; to get their prices down. Something comes over Frank when he shops in those outdoor markets. He sees it as a game that he has no intention of losing. I am sometimes embarrassed by his haggling techniques. Frank would walk away if they didn't "cooperate," but all the women knew each other well and they decided to have some fun with the stubborn American. They overheard me asking him to be reasonable. They knew his name and they had his number.

"C'mon, Frankeee! How do ya expect us to pay our bills? Be nice, Frankeee!"

"Be a good mon, don't be a bad mon. We have nice things for you, Frankeee." I just couldn't let them think Frank was a bad mon. A little frugal, maybe, but bad, no.

"Oh, Frank's a very good man and He loves God! Listen ladies, he left a business in New York to work for a prison ministry in Washington." Frank gave me a look.

He hates it when I tell people his condensed bio. My info on

Frank backfired.

"Frankeee! You're a Christian? How could you take advantage of your sistahs? God will not bless dat, Frankeee. Do da right thing, Frankeee!" By this time, the whole aisle knew Frankeee, the Frugal man of Faith. The woman who he "bargained" with the longest told him that her husband is in prison and that she is the sole support-er of their four children. Frank gave me another "look" as I pro-ceeded to pay her the full price for the shirts and beads. She blessed me and gave Frank a mini-sermon on giving and getting in God's economy. She knew the Word well, and she was *quite* articulate. I hugged her and wished her God's blessings. She gave me a book-mark and promised to pray for Prison Fellowship and asked if we would pray for her husband.

After our market bargaining spree we took our last walk along the beach and admired God's creation. We felt blessed, rested, connected, encouraged, and FULL—and we really missed the kids. We were ready to return to our life in these United States. The kids liked their tee-shirts and beads, and Capri called our bedroom from the phone in the basement and asked if she could sleep with us that night. No problem, mon.

B e at rest once more, O my soul, for the LORD has been good to you.

—Psalm 116:7

15

It's My Body and I'll Cry If I Want To

I t was the beginning of the new millennium and the new me, and the compliments started to flow:

My neighbor—*"You look MUCH better."*
My Pastor—*"Looks like the Lord's doing a work in you."*
My teenage daughter—*"Mother, I can put my arms around you."*
My son—*"Ma, you could do one of those commercials."*
My younger daughter—*"Mommy, you were never fat."*
My unexpected house guest—*"You look 5 years younger!"*
My mother-in-law—*"You have a waistline again."*
My UPS man—*"Hey, did you, ughhhh, do something?"*
My husband—*"Honey, you should buy all new underwear!"*

It was enough to swell a person's head—but not mine. After all, I had just gotten rid of the swelling in my stomach. Well, not all of it, but I'm getting there. It's personal, it's painful, it's pathetic, and I'm willing to open up and talk about it.

The year was 1982. I was a young, attractive 25 year old school teacher: Brunette, 5'6", 130 lbs. I walked down the wedding aisle with grace and confidence and dreams.

The year was 1992 and the dream to be a mom had turned into a bit of a nightmare. Our third precious little angel was born.

Although she arrived without incident, the first delivery left me with a C-section and an accidental bladder cut (6 inches wide) and the second delivery left me with an episiotomy the length of Long Island. The babies were all healthy and I'm still trying to forgive those doctors for the extra stitches. I had become a mature, 35 year old domestic engineer: Brunette (with aggressive roots), 5'6", 150 lbs. They hadn't invented the AB Cruncher back then. Of course, I would have gotten one. When that gizmo was finally introduced, it was too little, too late.

The year was 1997. Frank and I celebrated our 15th anniversary. I remember wearing an expensive girdle to the restaurant that night. My deeply sensitive husband assured me I was still beautiful from the neck up. (Yep, he really said that.) I was 40 years old, 5'6" and 160 lbs. I had managed to gain precisely 2 lbs. a year for 15 years. It wasn't very hard to do! I could have done an infomercial on the process:

"Ladies, are you tired of your thin, bony bodies? Try my new diet plan—'Fifteen Years to Fullness and Flab!' Follow these guidelines and watch the pounds pile on. Eat what you want, have a few kids, refuse to exercise, tell people it's "baby" fat, blame the demons from Italy, and you too, can have a fuller, flabbier figure in just fifteen years!

I guarantee it!!!"

Needless to say, it was time. Time to do something. I was scared. I figured out that if I continued my eating habits and gaining 2 lbs. a year, that by the time I was 70, I would be the size of an aunt from Brooklyn! A very frightening thought.

To appreciate my search for a leaner, healthier body, one must know the depths of negative attitudes I had toward diet and/or exercise. Exercise was unthinkable and diets were for the birds or women who ate like birds. These women never look joyful, there is always food left on their plates (such waste!), and they never moan or seem delirious when tasting certain dishes. I consulted with a few formerly full-figured females and got quite a varied list of diets. Naturally, I tried them all. I counted calories. I counted fat grams. I counted carbs. I counted sugar. I counted how many days I went without an Oreo. One man I know had his stomach stapled and a woman I know had her jaw wired shut—attractive for gossip control, but not for dieting. I tried liquid shakes, fat burning vitamins, and of course, the "seafood" diet. (You know what *that* is!) I never went to group support meetings and I never bought Richard Simmon's videos for fear that he would show up at my house with his film crew. After 6 months of starving and counting and going to bed hungry, I had lost a whopping 2 lbs. Incredible, but true.

I was ready to give up and accept my lot in life as a zaftig woman (hey—it was honorable during the Renaissance), but an enthusiastic Christian friend intervened and told me about this stuff called "Pulse" marketed by the Brain Garden Company out in the middle of Utah. Pulse? Brain Garden? Utah? Sounded like hippie, tree-hugging activity to me. He assured me it was kosher (not in the literal sense) and so I placed my order. Ten bags of Pulse for ten days. Twelve dollars a bag. The box arrived and I dubiously commenced my Pulse diet. Each bag had a sketch of young Daniel and his friends refusing the King's food and drink. The entire portion of Daniel 1:3-20 was printed on the back. Sure enough, there it was—in verse 12—*"Prove thy servants, I beseech thee, ten days; and let them give us pulse to eat and water to drink."* Bingo! Eureka! Voila! The stuff looked like duck droppings but it was actually chopped up dried fruits, nuts and grains. Ten bags and ten gallons of water in ten days—and I lost ten pounds. It was a piece of cake (well, not in the literal sense). Ten down, twenty to go.

Since no "extreme" diet is healthy for any extended period, I tried to eat moderately for the next six months. No weight loss. Then, I went on the eat-all-the-protein-you-want diet. I ate all the foods that supposedly cause heart attacks. I never read the book and I'm not sure how it works, but I lost ten pounds in three months. Twenty down, ten to go.

Almost six months passed and I had not shed another ounce. It was time for the "E" word (can't bring myself to say it). I've avoided it. I've dreaded it. I've ignored it. I've cringed at the thought of it. I researched E equipment and studied E advertisements. I tried to E in the den but to no avail. I was too self-conscious to E in public. My loving husband who now thinks I'm looking better from the neck down, accompanied me to a fitness store and we purchased a treadmill. I had done my homework and I was focused and the sale took eight minutes. The treadmill was delivered the next day. It's very nice. My kids wanted me to try it out right away. I explained that it was brand new and I didn't want to get any dirt marks or sweat on it. I convinced them we should read the manual front to back before pressing the ON button.

Statistics show that 90% of E equipment in American homes is unused. I vowed that would *never* happen with my new purchase. I worked hard and walked countless miles on that thing for the next six months and those last ten pounds came off. I haven't gotten on it in a year—but it makes a wonderful place to hang delicates and knits, so I feel it is indeed, being used. A small group of friendly pounds have returned for a visit, but I really don't want them to stay too long. I suppose it's time to clear the clothes off the treadmill and put the sneakers back on. After all, I *would* like to be around for grandchildren.

D iscipline yourself for the purpose of godliness; [which is] profitable for all things.
—1 Timothy 4:7b; 8a (NASB)

16

June Bugs... Me

June was a particularly exhausting month. The weekdays were full and the weekends overflowed. Auditions, rehearsals, and recitals. Tryouts, tournaments, and playoffs. Graduations, a church dedication, and Father's Day celebrations. I chaperoned sleepovers, camp outs, and field trips (including fifty-two blonde women to the Women of Faith Conference). The pace really started to bug me.

I am not sure how life in the Lofaro household got swept into the fast-lane. Even our weekends are "scheduled." There was a time when Saturdays used to comprise half of a weekend. As I recall— Saturday used to be a day of rest before the day of rest. Granted, there were a few chores and errands—but nothing that couldn't be accomplished by noontime. In the last couple of years, I have noticed that Saturdays are even busier than weekdays. And Saturdays in June are the worst!

What has gone wrong? I'll tell you what has gone wrong; the children started displaying musical talents, athletic prowess, and social skills. Maybe that diaper season wasn't so bad after all. I liked being able to locate all three of them within 90 seconds. Now, it often takes 90 minutes, and I'm not fond of the adjustment. This was our schedule on a Saturday in mid-June:

6:30 A.M.—I swipe at the blaring alarm.

6:45 A.M.—I read a bit and lift a prayer; mainly for myself.

7:10 A.M.—I leave the bed and circulate through the other bedrooms searching for bodies. Only the teenager is in her bed. She is in a coma-like state and does not respond to warm greetings or cold threats. I vow to return.

7:15 A.M.—I arrive in the kitchen. Soda cans, a popcorn bowl with black kernels, and cookie crumbs are strewn across counter, along with a half empty box of sugar cereal and a half gallon of milk which is warm to the touch. I follow the cereal trail to the basement where the twelve year old has spent the night. Since he is forbidden to watch TV during the week, he has been awake since 6 *A.M.* in order to watch every cartoon ever made. He is afraid to miss any and wields the remote almost as masterfully as his father. Remnants of other late night snacks are scattered hither and yon. I lecture—he straightens the room. I insist he pay for the now spoiled milk to teach a lesson. I vow to return.

7:25 A.M.—I visit the master bathroom and notice I've aged. The husband is *not* in the bed (he has promised to fly in from Detroit in time for the recital—bless his heart) but the cute nine year old *is*. She apparently spent the night but I never noticed.

7:30 A.M.—I return to the teenager's room with a cattle prod. It works. She enters the shower stall, grunting every step of the way.

7:35 A.M.—I shout down two flights for the boy to turn off the boob tube and come up. It works. He enters the other shower.

7:37 A.M.—I hug the little one and whisper sweet nothings and remind her what the day holds. She insists she still smells good from her last shower. She's mistaken, and I send her on her way.

8:00 A.M.—Miraculously, we have all showered and dressed. I defrost bagels and dispense them like a deck of cards.

8:10 A.M.—I get in the car with the rising middle schooler who is to report for a special math screening. The school officials tell us he's practically a genius, but we have a hard time believing it because we've seen him outside the classroom.

8:30 A.M.—I race back to the house to pick up the teenager and the youngest. Both girls must report to the concert hall across town where I drove them the night before for a dress rehearsal (while Frank sat in a fine Steakhouse with two ministry donors from Detroit).

9:05 A.M.—We arrive five minutes late and I show no remorse. The teenager is insulted.

9:30 A.M.—The piano recital begins and I find a seat with a decent angle for the camcorder.

9:45 A.M.—The husband appears in time for the little one's rendition of "Alouette."

10:20 A.M.—The teenager plays a piece on the piano and then sings a spiritual and the theme song from "Prince of Egypt." Doesn't seem like the same person who was one with her bed just three hours earlier. The master teacher tells the audience to watch for her on Broadway. (She'll *never* get to sleep early!)

10:35 A.M.—I inform the husband that the son needs to be picked up. He informs me he met with officials until very late and got up at 5 to catch a plane. I slip out.

10:45 A.M.—I pick up the math genius; was told the test results would be forthcoming.

11:00 A.M.—We return to the recital in time for fruit and donuts—only soggy ones remain.

11:20 A.M.—I leave the recital with the two girls and beat the two guys home by a minute.

11:50 A.M.—I drive the little one to the softball field, run to the party store for paper goods and call home to remind husband to drive son to soccer field to join his team (a.k.a. Gray Whales) by 12:30. I vow to return.

12:30 P.M.—I sit and cheer on our little Mickey Mantle. During one inning, she is the catcher and the protective gear is bigger than she is. When she falls to her knees, she can't get back up. A wonderful moment to capture on film but the camcorder battery dies.

1:20 P.M.—I leave game, pick up ice cream cake, and rush home to check on teenager who is having seven friends for her birthday. The highlighted activity is water gun wars with those modern toys that hold 25 gallons.

1:55 P.M.—I return to softball field where I find husband and son cheering on the Pythons whose cute pitcher has just struck out three batters. I apologize to the soccer son for not making it to his game and tell him he no longer has to pay for the milk. The game goes into extra innings and I pray they lose so we can all go to my friend's barbecue. They win and the playoff is scheduled for 4:00 that day. I'm sad.

2:30 P.M.—I arrive home again to find eight teenagers running dizzily around the lawn shooting long streams of water at one another and my windows. Pizza arrives and I gladly pay for it. I place it *outside* on the deck. The teens assemble and converse like adults. I'm intrigued.

3:30 P.M.—I rush the little softball player to the field for a warm-up and leave her there with the team. I vow to return.

3:45 P.M.—I arrive home in time to say something meaningful to the teenagers.

4:00 P.M.—The teenagers are all gone. The water guns were a hit—figuratively and literally. My favorite teen is happy.

4:05 P.M.—I gather the rest of the family in the Durango and rush to the soccer party—held at a nondescript chain restaurant. Husband is not happy. Son receives trophy, camcorder works again. I am happy. The Gray Whales celebrate their winning season. I eat cold fries, there's a big bug on the wall, I vow never to return.

4:40 P.M.—We leave the soccer celebration early and arrive at the softball field late. The youngest child is not happy. They are half way through the third inning.

5:35 P.M.—The Pythons lose and my husband is extremely happy. We won't have to spend Father's Day on a mosquito infested field.

5:45 P.M.—The softball coach gives out trophies and certificates while playing hard rock music from the seventies on his boom box. Pizza is delivered to the field. It was okay but I secretly yearn for the gourmet treats at my friend's party.

6:18 P.M.—All the nine-year-old girls (a.k.a. Pythons) walk over to the adjoining pool to go for a swim. All the nice parents follow behind. They seem happy.

6:38 P.M.—Our youngest is the first to be extracted from the pool, (by *her* nice parents). She objects. I then hunt for the other two children. This is no simple task but I accomplish it in under four minutes. I am no longer interested in who is happy.

7:00 P.M.—We arrive (three hours late) at the surprise 40th birthday party. Only three people are left and the food has either been eaten or put away. We stay twenty minutes. The host seems happy when we leave.

7:30 P.M.—We arrive home and our children inform us the night is young. I feel an urge to vow never to return anywhere. (That is when I considered vacationing alone.)

7:55 P.M.—Instead, I take a long, hot shower, put on pajamas, and I serve cold milk and warm cookies.

8:30 P.M.—We do a lot of dunking and we watch a classic movie and we talk about the busy day and everybody seems pretty happy. I suppose we could all really use a good vacation. Let the summer begin!

10:05 P.M.—I load the milk glasses into the dishwasher and press the start button. Husband locks up the house

10:15 P.M.—Another shower to remove the smell of playing fields and greasy fries.

10:30 P.M.—Good night hugs and a very brief family prayer.

Lord, thank you for abilities, for opportunities, and for privileges. Thank you for health to run and sing and eat and play. Thank you for community and people who have invested in our lives. Help us to be good representatives of your Kingdom. Show us your ways. Help us to remember the big difference between happiness and joy. Forgive our grumbling. Have mercy on us when we fail. We love you.

His divine power has given us everything we need for life and godliness through our knowledge of him who called us *by his own glory and goodness.*

—2 Peter 1:3

17

Nothing But the Truth

I t was the fall of 1975, and I was a happy college freshman. Two months into the first semester, I was happy about my courses, my professors, my decision to be a high school English teacher, my new friends, and my all-girls dorm. I was happy about my diet of subs, pizza, and ice cream. I was happy to be at Boston College, on a beautiful campus, and in God's will. And I was happy when the Campus Crusade for Christ staff brought a speaker named Josh McDowell to the campus to discuss God, truth, and—uh—sex.

The Christian students who entered McHugh Forum that night were eager to hear a middle-aged man (he was 35) speak about the topic with intelligence and without prudishness. The non-believers who attended were eager to hear what a father of four could possibly have to say that made any sense. Those riding the fence were eager for any reasonable treatise. Besides, it was free.

The non-celebrity guest speaker was energetic, eloquent and emphatic. He spoke with great authority, not only because his summations were grounded in the Word of God, but also because they were supported by facts. The guy was a walking statistics file. What I did not know at the time was that he had written *Evidence That Demands a Verdict* just three years earlier. That book has been reprinted dozens of times, and it is the most quoted book of all time in regard to Christian apologetics. Every home should have one.

Fast forward exactly 27 years. We spent a week at the Sandy Cove Christian Conference Center on the beautiful shores of North East, Maryland. It was a terrific week of relaxation, water sports, and edification. The guest speaker for all five nights was, you guessed it, Josh McDowell. Imagine the thrill of attending a family retreat to hear a speaker who had impacted my life so many years ago.

The now-celebrity guest speaker is still energetic, eloquent, and emphatic. His hair is silver, he is just a bit past middle age (he is 62), and he now speaks with abandonment, passion, and urgency. He makes no apologies for his straight talk. He pleads with parents and grandparents of "born again, fundamental, church-going young people" to get their heads out of the sand. He insists we are "in trouble" and he has documentation to substantiate every word. Mr. McDowell has written 82 books and he is about to launch a website called BeyondBelief.com.

He was quite animated as he described this cutting edge site as "an intersection, NOT a destination." This is a man who understands God's economy of time.

Josh is still asking the same questions he was asking 30 years ago. To his dismay, fewer people are responding with the correct answers. Several times he left the platform and came down the center aisle to ask questions of people (young and old) in the audience of 1000. The answers weren't stupid—they were just incorrect.

Why is lying wrong?
What determines moral reality?
Are family values reliable?
Is it allowable to judge others according to Matthew 7:1?
Is killing wrong?
What is the purpose of sex?
Is the New Testament historically accurate?
Can the resurrection be proven?
Is the Bible from God?
How can the Bible be trusted?
Why is Christianity the only path to heaven?
How do you know Moses wrote the Pentateuch?
What difference does it make who wrote it?

Why do so many scholars say the gospels are unreliable?
Where are the original manuscripts?
Why didn't Jesus say he was God?

I don't know about you, but I didn't do too well. By the way, if your answer to the first question is "cause the Bible tells me so," Josh says you're wrong. For all the correct answers, buy his book!

Yes, the Holy Bible is the authoritative, final word in the life of the believer, but we have not done our homework. Another great author in the area of apologetics is Paul Little. Just as the titles suggest—*Know What You Believe* and *Know Why You Believe*—his books are equivocal to Christianity 101 but, sadly, most Christians are unable to articulate their content. Forget the theatre tickets, the Gameboy, and the new sweater from Gap. Do yourself and the kids in your life a great favor and read some of these books together. It's an investment that will bless you one hundred fold.

In the eight years that Frank served on the leadership team of Prison Fellowship Ministries, we had many occasions to be in the company of our dear friend, Chuck Colson. He is considered one of the greatest Christian thinkers of our time. His passion for "Christian world-view" has sparked many thousands of people toward a more dynamic witness. Once the Chief Counsel to President Nixon, this former convict has delighted the church, astounded his critics, and quieted the likes of Larry King.

Why? The answer is double-edged. I have heard words such as "genius, brilliant, intellectual, and great statesman" often used to describe Chuck. And I believe that all to be true. What is highly unfortunate is that the Christian culture seems so desperate for the few "heroes" who have been successful, respected, educated, articulate, and "powerful" in Christ. Secular adversaries of the Christian faith often (and successfully) attack our ranks because of the lack of arsenal in our fortresses. The credibility of modern Christianity often suffers because of the lack of credibility of modern Christians.

Chuck Colson, Josh McDowell, Ravi Zacharias, Kay Arthur, John MacArthur, Chuck Smith, and Beth Moore are all wonderful communicators. I admire each one but I don't want to depend on them. I want to be more knowledgeable of the Bible myself. I want to be able to intelligently explain my faith. I want to enter any conversation with any person in any setting and provide a ready defense for my beliefs.

And oh, how I want all that for my children and—Lord willing—for my grandchildren.

John 8:32 tells us *"You will know the truth and the truth will set you free."* Millions of Christian believers have been martyred in the past twenty centuries. May the truth they lived for and died for be fully learned so that we can compassionately teach it to a world in search of meaning.

D o your best to present yourself to God as one approved, a workman who does not need to be ashamed and who correctly handles the word of truth.

—2 Timothy 2:15

18

Parent Traps

Kermit the Frog used to lament, "It's not easy being green." I'm sure he had his reasons, but I'd like Kermit to know that it's not any easier being a parent. Parents have felt this way since the fourth chapter of Genesis, and things have become trickier ever since. The twenty-first century has brought an astounding number of challenges to parenthood. Let's just say there are serious "land mines" that await us each day.

Take, for instance, the whole topic of homework. I didn't mind homework too much as a student, but as a parent, I have come to loathe it. You see, I was born around the middle of the last century and so, many facets of my children's homework is, well … new. They have new spelling and new history and new math. After I cleaned up the dinner dishes the other night, my daughter asked me to help her with her math homework. I hesitantly obliged and it wasn't long before she was in tears. She told me I was dividing wrong and adding wrong and that if she did the work my way, the teacher would mark it wrong. Advanced algebra? Nope—just fractions with a fourth grader!

Carpooling is another phenomenon which our mothers knew not of. My mother didn't even apply for a driver's license until she was middle aged. She knew exactly what she was doing—that sly fox. On Mondays alone, I pick up Paris at school, and then I pick up Capri, and then I drop them off for piano and voice lessons. I run to pick up Jordan to get him to soccer on time. I pick up his friend, whose mother works, and then I leave the soccer field to run and get the girls. You should see me on Saturdays. I'm actually thinking of decorating the inside of the SUV since I spend so much time in it.

Computers are another source of frustration and failure, and they do indeed affect my ability to parent. I was helping Capri add sub-sentences to her report and I inadvertently deleted her report. When Jordan asked me to set up margins (I could do it quite well on my electric typewriter), I erased the left half of his essay and never found it again. Paris' theater teacher sends attachments that I cannot locate. I am quite sure there's a huge attachment file floating between my house and Mars with lots of stuff waiting for me.

The kids cannot believe that I grew up without a computer. I assured them the first computer I ever saw was in a sci-fi movie with "2001" in its title—it was a far-off year and a far-flung premise, and I was confident at age 13 that neither would ever come to pass. The computer was named Hal, and as I recall, it had a mind of its own.

The computer was not the only thing we lived without in the last century. "Ma! You didn't have calculators? VCRs? Microwaves? Fax machines? CD players? Game Boys? Nintendos? DVDs? Play Stations? Game Cubes? How did you live? What was that like? Did you feel deprived? What did you do for fun?"

"Well, I had a nifty eight track player in junior high—oh, never mind."

I really felt old recently when a friend came for lunch and brought along her preschooler. After the four-year-old little sweetie finished her sandwich, I offered to set her up in the TV room to watch a cartoon on our new DVD player. She propped herself up on the couch and I covered her cherub-like legs with a quilt. I looked around and located three separate remote controls. Surely one would work. I pressed 73 buttons and nothing worked. I pointed them at the TV, the DVD, the VCR, and finally, at my frazzled brain. The little angel popped off the couch.

"I'll do it!" She relieved me of all three and within 15 seconds, she clicked on the TV, clicked over to the DVD and clicked up the volume. Humbled yet again.

A friend of mine told me a great story related to the huge land mine of being discriminating and discerning about family entertainment. A father of three teenagers had a family rule that they could not attend "R" rated movies. His teens wanted to see a particular popular movie that had just been released in local theaters. It was rated "R."

The teens interviewed friends and even some members of their church to find out what was offensive or questionable in the movie. They made a list of pros and cons about the movie in order to convince their dad that they should be allowed to see it.

The cons? It contained only three curse words, the only violence was a building exploding (and that's on TV all the time), and you actually did not "see" the couple in the movie having physical relations; it was just implied—off camera, of course.

The pros? It was a very popular movie—a true blockbuster! Everyone was seeing it. It contained a good story and a good plot. It had some great adventure and suspense. There were some brilliant special effects. The stars were some of the most talented actors in Hollywood. It probably would be nominated for several awards. Many of the members of their Christian church had seen the movie and said it "wasn't too bad." If they could see the movie then they would not feel like "rejects" when their peers discussed it.

Since there were more pros than cons, the teens had asked their father to reconsider his position just this ONE time and let them have permission to go see it. The father looked at the list and thought for a few minutes. He told them he could see they put considerable time and thought into their request. He asked if he could have a day to think about things before making his decision.

The three teenagers were thrilled. They were sure that they "had him" because their arguments were so convincing. There was no way Dad could turn them down. They happily agreed to let him have a day to think about their request. The next evening, the father called his three teenagers, who were smiling smugly, into the living room. There, on the coffee table, he had placed a plate of brownies. His kids were puzzled. The father told them he had thought about their request and had decided that if they would each eat a brownie, then he would let them go to the movie. But—just like the movie, the brownie had pros and cons.

The pros? They were made with the finest chocolate and other premium quality ingredients. They had the added delight of yummy chocolate chips in them. The brownies were moist and fresh with wonderful, smooth, creamy, luscious chocolate frosting on top.

He had made these fantastic brownies using an award winning recipe. And best of all, the brownies had been lovingly made by the hands of their own dear father.

The cons? The brownies had only one. He had included a special ingredient. The brownies also contained just a little bit of dog poop. But he had mixed it in well and they probably would not even be able to taste the dog poop. He baked the brownies at 350 degrees, so any bacteria or germs had probably been destroyed.

Therefore, if any of his children could stand to eat the special brownies which included "just a little bit of crap" and not be affected by it—then he was confident they would also be able to see the movie with "just a little bit of smut" and not be affected.

Of course, none of them would eat the brownies and the smug smiles left their faces as they filed out of the room. Now when his teenagers ask permission to do something that involves questionable content, the father just asks, "Would you like me to whip up a batch of my special brownies?" There are never any takers.

Parenting ... it's not just a job ... it's an adventure. May God be our guide.

C ome, my children, listen to me; I will teach you the fear of the LORD.

—Psalm 34:11

19

Who Moved the Chairs?

For me, the highlight of the 2001 Christmas season was the third annual "Evening in December." This gathering (which I helped birth) was held in beautiful downtown Reston. The setting was lovely, the weather delightful, and the invitations were classy and embossed. They were hand delivered by the fifty women who were then attending the weekly Bible study I teach. Some of these precious women are very new to the practice of studying God's Word, but they are already obeying the commission to "Go and tell!"

The invitation promised bountiful desserts, festive ambience, and lots of women. I believe the latter ingredient was the strongest draw. Women need women. Women understand women. Women comfort women. Women resonate with all those hormonal issues, not to mention the demands of "creating" Christmas. In some homes, the woman is the producer, director, social secretary, accountant, and caterer of all that the Christmas season entails. This particular annual gathering is a way of strengthening our sense of community, making women feel special, and most importantly, it is a time to come away from the hustle and bustle to hear about the true meaning of Christmas. God so loved the world that He gave the greatest gift of all. Have you received Him? Have you made Him your own? Do you know Him, or do you simply know about Him?

Three years earlier, we held the first such party at my friend Janice's house. Besides being the mother of two active boys, she is the wife of a former NFL player, and an incredibly gifted interior decorator who dresses her house (inside and out) "to the nines" at Christmas. Over one hundred women attended. The following year, the RSVP's doubled, and so we moved the gathering to the property of Prison Fellowship Ministries. (That's the ministry responsible for "causing" me to move away from Long Island.)

The first hour was spent mingling and enjoying sumptuous desserts in the gracious DeMoss House, a grand and historic century-old home, which is the centerpiece of the ministry's property. We then guided the ladies into the brisk night air, past the porch, down the back steps, along the path, and into the large multi-purpose room of the PFM office complex. To add to the challenge, over fifty women attended the event who had not sent RSVP's. The abundant dessert buffet lasted but the cold punch and hot cider did not. The enthusiastic hostesses remained unruffled. When we directed the two hundred-plus attendees toward the meeting room for the presentation, it became immediately clear that we were in a bind concerning the shortage of seats. The hostesses promptly scattered up and down the hallways that flanked the large meeting room and returned with chairs—lots of chairs—about two dozen. These were not folding chairs, but rather desk chairs. All upholstered, all tweed blue, all on rollers, all seemingly alike.

After some Christmas humor and a couple of soothing solos by my friend Tina, I shared the true meaning of the season and invited our guests to consider taking a step toward God through prayer and Bible study. The response cards caused rejoicing in heaven and in all those who supported the effort. We gave away door prizes, sang a couple of carols and sent our grateful guests out with a reminder of the Lord's perfect love. When the crowd thinned out, a small group straightened out the meeting room and returned the chairs to the offices. Another group returned to the DeMoss House to tidy up and unplug the seasonal lights. I slept well that Monday night. I knew that if nothing else was to transpire, the gift of Christmas had arrived and I was the recipient. As I passed into a deeper sleep, my final thought focused on a Proverb—"The desire accomplished is sweet to the soul." I had surely tasted God's sweetness that night.

The alarm clock rang much too early, as it does every day. I made the beds (well, just my bed), did the laundry (actually, just one load of towels), and served my fourth grader a hot breakfast (okay, so it was a Pop Tart with Nesquik). My "baby" headed to the bus stop and I had thirty minutes to collect my notes and shower before the 9:30 A.M. Bible study. I was concluding our twelve week journey in Philippians, the Epistle of Joy. Fittingly, we had all experienced a measure of pure joy just the night before. Talk about a sermon illustration! I was about to put on my socks when the phone rang at 9 sharp. I picked up and it was the Senior Vice-President of Prison Fellowship Ministries, who also happened to be my husband. Surely he was calling to celebrate all God had done the evening before. I got home late and we didn't have time to catch up.

"Hi Frank, did you get any feedback about last night?" I was fishing for a compliment.

"Hi Ellie. Yes, as a matter of fact I did."

"Really, what did you hear? Will they let us use the building again next year?"

"I don't think so." I was stunned.

"Why not? What happened? It was a terrific night."

"Ellie, have you ever heard of a little book called *Who Moved My Cheese?*"

"Yep, heard about it but never read it. What's the point?"

"The author wrote a simple parable that reveals profound truths. Cheese is used as a metaphor for what we want in life. In the story, the characters are faced with unexpected change. We are creatures of habit and comfort and people generally dislike change."

"No offense, Frank, but you're gonna have to land the plane. I'm going to be late for Bible study. Surely you are not calling about cheese!"

"Over twenty people in IT (computer geniuses, I think) arrived to work this morning to find their chairs either in the halls or in the wrong cubicles and they are NOT happy."

"What's the big deal? They all look alike."

"They are NOT all alike. Those chairs become contoured to your body. There are inter-office memos going around the building about the rude group that rearranged the furniture. You better get down here and do some damage control. Apologies are needed."

"Are you serious, Frank?"

"Highly. You better get here fast and you better be humble."

"Does this mean you'll never be promoted?"

"You're not funny, Ellie."

"Just shootin' for a little joy. Thanks for the call. See you after Bible study." Click.

I arrived at the sanctuary five minutes late that Tuesday morning and before I began to teach, I commended all the women concerning their selfless giving and the blessings of God that cannot be contained. I decided not to mention the late night office break-in that resulted in "Chairgate" (sorry Chuck Colson). After wrapping up the study (be anxious for nothing), I went directly to the supermarket to buy four dozen "homemade" cookies.

It was now noontime and I planned to serve them to all the computer people and anyone else whose cheese was moved. And I planned to be humble.

"Aren't you Ellie Lofaro?" an older lady asked. She had a strong southern accent, a salad to go, and she was ahead of me on the express line.

"Yes I am. Do I know you?"

"My name is Andrea. I work at Prison Fellowship."

"Well, that's funny, I'm heading right over there with these cookies. I helped to organize a Christmas event last night and it seems we had a little trouble with unhappy mice—uh, I mean—people in IT."

"I know all about your Christmas party. I work in IT. We got an e-mail about it this morning. I'm one of the people who spent a half hour trying out chairs looking for the right one."

Frank said to be humble ... Frank said to be humble ... Frank said to be humble ...

"I am SO sorry about moving your chair. We really didn't mean any harm."

Andrea paid for her salad and leaned back toward my cookies. "Dear, I want you to know that I consider it an honor for a local woman to sit in MY chair in order to hear the Good News of

Christmas. Isn't that what it's all about?"

I realized I had found a new best friend and so I handed Andrea my cell phone. "Could you please call my husband? He needs your perspective on cheese."

She asked a few more questions and was genuinely joyful about how God had moved in so many lives. I told her 51 women signed up to join our Bible study and asked her to keep our group in her prayers. I arrived at PF a half hour later and to my surprise, Andrea had circulated an e-mail throughout the entire building. A friend of mine at the ministry later forwarded it to me:

> *From:* *Andrea Mason*
> *Sent:* *Tuesday, December 11, 2001*
> *To:* *All Reston PF Staff*
> *Subject:Was your chair missing this morning?*
>
> *Well, if you were one of the fortunate ones who did not have a chair at your desk when you came in this morning, then praise God for that and tell Him thank you! Praise God that so many women committed to studying the Bible and that we were able to use our chairs to allow all who came to hear the GOOD NEWS! And praise Him for the problem of too many people coming out to hear about Jesus.*

By the time I arrived at PF with the cookies, Andrea's e-mail and the entire episode was local legend. I was well received by every mouse I met. One young man confessed, "I was ticked off at first but now I'm kind of embarrassed for getting so twisted out of shape over a chair." I remembered Frank's admonition to be humble.

"Yes, you are SO right."

Often we have little control over the cheese-movers in our lives. What we can control is how we respond. I don't like cheese-moving any better than anyone else. But God didn't call us to be comfortable. What I can't control, I can embrace—if I remember that all things are working together for the good of those who love Him. It may not be evident at first what that good is, and the good may not be for me alone. but what God has promised, He is faithful to bring about when we trust Him.

So, ... do not be anxious for your life, as to what you shall eat, or what you shall drink, nor for your body as to what you shall put on it (OR WHERE YOU SHALL SIT IT). Seek first the Kingdom of God ... and all things shall be added to you (Matthew 6:25, 33, a tiny bit paraphrased).

T herefore do not worry about tomorrow, for tomorrow will worry about itself. Each day has enough trouble of its own.

—Matthew 6:34

20

The (Almost) Good Mother

I t was a typical Wednesday night. Frank was working late because he feels called to donate extra time to the ministry. (My theory is that he doesn't want to get involved with the carpool issues). We inhaled dinner, brushed our teeth, and jumped in the Durango. I drove to one church where Jordan and Capri attend AWANA—a wonderful Bible memorization program for children, and then to another church, where Paris attends ONEIGHTY—an innovative outreach where teenagers are inundated with junk food, video games, loud music, and Jesus. (Let's just say it's not your grandmother's mid-week prayer service).

I then drove to the local Marriott Residence Inn with its lovely living room with plenty of couches, tables, and chairs. I arrive there each Wednesday evening at 7:15 and sit at the table in the back right corner, as far away as possible from the suspended T.V. perpetually tuned to CNN. By the time I get there, the hotel guests interested in freebies have left the premises after enjoying burgers, dogs, chips, and cookies. I always greet the kind young Guatemalan woman who vacuums the earth tone room. I proceed to empty my tote bag onto the square dining table. Out come two Bibles, one concordance, a study guide by Warren Wiersbe, and a notebook. I reach into my handbag for a blue pen, a black pen, a red Flair, and a yellow Hi-liter. I bow my head, say a prayer, reach for my tools and proceed to prepare the lesson I will share with local Reston women each week. I plan to expound upon the biblical text of Ephesians 2, and I will spend a great deal of time on the nature and beauty and privilege of "inheritance."

On that particular Wednesday evening, I had a breakthrough with the Holy Spirit and I began to write with passion, conviction, and direction. I felt enlightened and inspired and then my cell phone rang.

"Mrs. Lofaro?"

"Speaking."

"This is Janice Lane, Capri's group leader at AWANA. She slipped and fell during gametime and is unable to put any pressure on her left foot. We have ice on it, but you will probably want to come over and get her." My thoughts scurried.

It was only 7:45. AWANA is not over until 8:45. I am supposed to have another hour to finalize this lesson. I will probably want to come over? What if I probably don't want to come over? What if I definitely don't want to come over? What if I want to be alone? What if I want a break? What if I'm tired of having my plans rearranged by short people?

"Is my little honey in pain?"

"No, she's actually taking it like a champ. No tears or complaints."

The Marriott is only five minutes from the church that hosts AWANA, which is why I go there instead of driving home. The 90 minutes of study time is just perfect. I need that time. Really, I do. I doubted Capri suffered more than a simple sprain.

"Thank you so much for calling. Please tell Capri I love her and that I'll be there as soon as I can—probably, um, uh ... about 20 minutes."

"Okay. We'll see you then. Bye-bye."

Well, at least I bought myself 15 more minutes. After all, I was on a spiritual roll. I jotted down two more sentences, felt my stomach tighten, and decided I was a horrible mother. I placed the key into the ignition two minutes later. When I arrived at the church, I was led down two hallways and into a small room where my then nine-year-old baby girl sat atop a desk. She gave me a half grin, mostly because she was enjoying all the attention.

"Can you walk on it honey?"

"No way."

"Can you try?"

"Nope, I already tried. It's broken."

"Capri! Don't say that! It's not broken."

"Ma ... did you forget? When it doesn't swell ... it's broken."

"It's probably just a bad sprain. We'll call Dr. Thal in the morning."

I thanked the people who cared for Capri and proceeded to carry her through the halls, past the large crowd (where I used contorted facial gestures to extract Jordan), up the stairs, and across the parking lot. It dawned on me that the pip-squeak of the family was no longer light. Night passed and morning came and I learned that our neighbor, Dr. Ray Thal (from Long Island), was away on vacation. His associate could not see Capri until 1:00. I drove her to school, carried her into the nurse's office and placed her in a pre-arranged wheelchair. Jordan strolled off with his little sister, and she beamed as if she were a bride walking down the aisle. Everyone stared, and many offered sympathy, gifts, and favors. She rode the elevator all day, got excused from P.E., and received a free ice cream from the lunch lady. Capri was one happy camper.

I made it to the morning Bible study on time but not on target. The teacher was not fully prepared. I greeted the women and opened with a simple prayer. We all turned to chapter 2 of Ephesians and a volunteer began to read aloud. She read verses 1-7, and then another woman read:"For it is by grace you have been saved, through faith—and this not from yourselves, it is the gift of God—not by works, so that no one can boast. For we are God's workmanship, created in Christ Jesus to do good works, which God prepared in advance for us to do" (Ephesians 2:8-10).

Mmmm ... "which God prepared in advance for us to do" ... as believers, our works are not only good, they are prepared. What an amazing concept! In Ephesians 1, we learn of our riches in Christ. He has chosen us, adopted us, accepted us, redeemed us, forgiven us, revealed God's will to us, and arranged our inheritance. A friend of mine just adopted a Chinese baby girl who was abandoned with a note pinned to her blanket. This friend happens to be quite wealthy and I was struck by the fact that this little girl became wealthy the minute those adoption papers were signed. She didn't earn it, or work for it, or even ask for it. But everything they have is now hers.

How bankrupt we are when we do not know our inheritance. We are wealthy in Christ's riches, and yet many of us live as spiritual paupers. I am sad for the times I spend looking toward my duties rather than God's delight. Paul balances doctrine with duty. We inherit the wealth by faith and invest the wealth by works. The point of the lesson suddenly became clear to me and I was filled with tears. I shared about my week and the incidents that were causing resentment, frustration, exhaustion, and burnout. I explained that we need to serve the Lord with a joyful heart and do all things (even the menial, mundane tasks) as unto the Lord. I shared about how badly I had missed the mark that week. I shared about how duty becomes a joy-buster when our motives are not in line with God's will. The Bible study didn't go as I had expected that morning—how often God exceeds our expectations.

I picked up Capri (literally) from school and got to the orthopedic specialist at 1:00 sharp. Three x-rays and two hours later, she was the proud owner of a purple cast and two chrome crutches. When the doctor came in with the bad news, Capri let out a celebratory holler. The kid was beaming with pride. She couldn't wait to get to school the next day, or to church that Sunday, or back to AWANA the following Wednesday. She absolutely reveled in her new personal chauffer service (moi) to and from school for three weeks. I bought her a new Easter dress with purple flowers to match the cast, and she made sure everyone noticed her "condition." Of course, I was the one to wash that leg, that foot, and those toes when the cast came off. I suppose it was a good work that God prepared in advance.

Oh, the depth of the riches of the wisdom and knowledge of God!
—Romans 11:33

21

The DMV Blues

When Dante Alighieri penned his epic, *Inferno*, I'm convinced he had some sort of supernatural futuristic visions of the chamber of horrors we now call the Department of Motor Vehicles. I have never had an enjoyable experience at the DMV. I have no fond memories of the DMV. I can't say I am a fan of the DMV. More pointedly, I dislike the DMV.

Oh, I understand the need for such a place. I realize somebody has to keep track of the data. I appreciate the fact that monitoring millions of licenses, permits, tickets, tests and the like is no easy task. And I'm sure many employees of the DMV are frustrated by continuous budget cuts. It's quite possible that they, too, dislike the DMV.

Here in Virginia, the Governor made serious fiscal adjustments and recently closed many DMV offices across the state. That was curious since the lines were already longer than the ones in Disney World. Our oldest child, Paris, turned fifteen and one half. The "one half" is key, since that entitles her to take a test in order to receive a learner's permit. The learner's permit entitles her to drive with an experienced driver at her side. The experienced driver at her side, would be, more often than not, yours truly.

Paris was eligible to take the test in mid-November, so, in mid-September, she started pleading to "stop by" the DMV to pick up the instructions and study guide in order to be prepared for the big day. I tried to explain to her that there is no such thing as just being able to "stop by" the DMV. One month passed, and I decided to be kind and humble and to demonstrate unconditional love to my firstborn. I summoned courage and energy and I drove Paris to the DMV.

We waited on a long, snake-shaped line that ended at a sterile information booth. (In literature, the "snake-shaped line" would be referred to as "foreshadowing.") The booth was occupied by a young woman with no facial expression and an armed security guard (also expressionless) who looked ready, willing, and able to subdue anyone whose facial or verbal expressions got too expressive.

Ninety-four minutes after arriving at the DMV in the town of Sterling, we reached the head of the line. I hoped our encounter would be short and sweet. It was neither. I told the receptionist Paris' age and last name and asked for the instructional booklet and an application. As if there were a blinking arrow over my head, she entered our last name in her computer and proceeded to advise me that my own license would expire at the end of the month—October 31 to be exact. She proceeded to hand me my very own booklet and application. Paris seemed to enjoy the whole experience.

"Mom, this is great. Maybe you could fail and then take the test again in November with me. We could take it together. It would be a special mother-daughter bonding experience."

"Paris, first of all, I have no intention of failing and second of all, that's not my idea of bonding, and third of all—I don't even know why my license is expiring. I'm a middle-aged woman with a flawless driving record."

"What about the speeding ticket you got on the way to pick up Jordan at his new school last month?"

"Oh yeah, I forgot."

"And that parking ticket in D.C.?"

"That was Daddy's fault."

"Mother, a good driver takes responsibility for his or her choices."

Kids say the darndest things.

"Well, it was flawless for forty-five years!"

"You haven't been driving forty-five years."

"You know what I meant. Get in the car, Paris."

"Can I drive?"

"Nice try ... maybe next month."

Two weeks passed and I made my way back to the same DMV office. There was a sign posted on the door announcing that it was permanently closed. I peeked through the window. No line. No information booth. No long counter. Nobody. Nothing. Amazing!

And frustrating. I got back in the car and proceeded another twenty minutes west to Leesburg. The line wasn't too long and the woman at the information booth actually smiled. She assigned me a number and told me to have a seat. Two hours later, my number was called by the same female voice at airports. I submitted my application, took a vision test, and was told to sit and wait to be called for the actual test. Ten minutes passed and I was assigned to cubicle 13. The computer greeted me by my name and gave me a couple a fun practice questions. The test consists of all multiple-choice questions. Ten road signs are shown and you must identify all ten correctly. If that is achieved, there are then twenty-five general questions. You can skip a question but you must answer at least twenty of them correctly. I expected to sail smoothly.

I was on sign number six when the computer informed me I was incorrect and bid me farewell. I felt like a game show loser. Ellie Lofaro, you are the weakest link! There was no one to complain to, nowhere to hide, no judge to hear an appeal. Even so, I returned to the main counter.

"Excuse me sir, I failed Part One."

"Yes, I know. I saw you being terminated."

"The sign with the big bicycle threw me off. I thought it meant yield to the bicycle."

"Obviously, you were wrong."

"Sir, when can I take the test again?"

"Your license expires the last day of October, so I suggest you return tomorrow if you do not want to be arrested for driving without one."

It was humbling to announce my "news" at dinner that evening.

Frank and the kids laughed and Paris seemed to take great joy in my failure. I studied three hours that night and returned the following day, which happened to be Halloween. More lines, more waiting, more anxiety. I was assigned to test cubicle 7 and felt a sweat come over my brow. To add to the drama, an elderly woman dressed like a witch was in cubicle 6, and a full-figured "bunny" with ears wriggled into cubicle 8. It was a bad dream, but at least it had a happy ending; I left with a new license.

Two weeks later, I returned with an excited, well-prepared, confident teenager. She failed. I tried to console her without a smirk or a sermon. Unlike adults, teens must wait two weeks for a retest. We returned after Thanksgiving. The temperature was below 30 and the line was out the door. When I peeked inside, I noted the lobby was empty and the seating area was only half full. The armed guard let ten people in at a time. Somehow, it felt like we were being subjected to an evil regime in a Communist country. We finally made it inside after losing all feeling in our fingers and toes.

Paris passed with flying colors, and she gleefully drove home at dusk. During dinner, family conversation focused on pride and humility, success and failure, expectations and realities. My pride often keeps me from sharing my failures and my expectations often result in disappointment. I was reminded how important it is for family and friends to see my shortcomings as well as my strengths. I'm quite adept at displaying my strengths. How much more healthy we would all be if we stopped "posing."

A relative recently told me that I make her feel spiritually inferior. I quickly decided that was her problem, and the Lord quickly showed me it was mine. I pray to be more humble, more transparent, and more approachable. Pure love has no counterfeits. I met the DMV's requirements. I deeply desire to do the same with God's.

I can't wait until Paris turns 16. I may never go grocery shopping again. Goodbye, Dante's *Inferno* and hello, Milton's *Paradise*.

B e completely humble and gentle; be patient, bearing with one another in love.

—Ephesians 4:2

22

7 to 7

My husband Frank has an old fashioned work ethic. That's a nice way of saying he doesn't easily allow himself to stop and smell the flowers. When I married him, he owned three cafes—each had a delightful Victorian motif with a live vocalist performing top forty love songs while strumming a mellow guitar. Patrons lingered over fondues, stuffed breads, and popular board games. Frank circulated through the three locations by night and did accounting, purchasing, quality control, and staff training by day. The hours were grueling, and fortunately for our marriage, the restaurants were sold one year after the wedding.

When he decided to attend law school, we met for dinner three nights a week (fine with me) and he spent weekends in the library or curled up on the living room couch with a legal brief *(not fine with me)*. He never took the bar exam and never had any intention to practice law. He simply wanted the education. *Isn't that special?* In those carefree, childfree years, I did *more* important things with my free time ... I just can't seem to remember what they were.

When Frank completed his MBA and purchased a manufacturing company, I had high hopes that he would slow down a bit and enjoy being the boss. (So, what's wrong with resting on one's laurels?) No such thing with this guy. After all, this was his big chance to put his economics acumen, his business management skills, and his legal education to work all at once. I made babies and he made money, and his twelve hour work days (only six hours on Saturdays) were the norm for seven years. When I protested, he informed me that, *"most men in America are away from the house from 7 A.M. to 7 P.M. In other countries, the workday is even longer. You should be grateful for the opportunities the business has afforded us. We need to make money while we're able. We work hard but we also play hard. The kids will be able to go to college. You'll be set when I die."* Yada, yada, yada.

Then, in 1994, the most unsettling thing happened. Frank became a zealot. He was reading his Bible every day and keeping a journal of spiritual goals. He was grappling with what Bob Buford, author of *Halftime*, refers to as "the transition from success to significance." The rap group DCTalk wrote a song about Frank called "Jesus Freak."

Yessiree, that was my husband. He was doing crazy things like putting the house and the business and the lawn mower up for sale. Why did he have to take Isaiah 6:8 so literally? Sure, I had prayed for him to grow in wisdom and stature and to deepen in his faith and devotion, but couldn't he do all that in New York? After all, there are plenty of sinners in New York! Surely God could find something for Frank to do in New York! Little did I realize that the answer to my prayers would spell *"Hello, full-time-ministry"* and *"Bye-bye, New York."*

After seeking the Lord and the counsel of the wise, Frank agreed to accept a position with Prison Fellowship Ministries, which was founded by Chuck Colson and located outside Washington, D.C. I had two months in which to say my good-byes and find some sense of closure to spending 37 years within a 30-mile radius. At a farewell brunch with the church ladies, my last words were, "Please pray for me. I don't really have a heart for prisoners. I think they should be in prison." Yet another lesson in the many ways one can prepare (and eat) humble pie. Actually, I spend a good deal of time eating that particular pie. Some ex-convicts are now very close friends.

As Frank's responsibilities at Prison Fellowship Ministries grew, his devotion to prisoners and their families grew as well. Frank still works 7 to 7 and goes in every Saturday morning. I don't know why I ever thought his work ethic would change just because he signed on with a non-profit ministry. There is no longer a financial impetus, the thrill of the deal is a thing of the past, and looming deadlines seem unnecessary. But Frank reminds me of the statistics and relates amazing testimonies and I eat more pie. After all, God deserves the very best we have to offer.

I am sitting on a beach chair intermittently writing this and staring at the ocean—my favorite vista on the planet. We are vacationing on the Outer Banks of North Carolina and our two-week getaway is coming to an end. During the first week, Frank answered cell phone calls, received and shot off e-mails, and flew to PF headquarters for a day—not exactly activities that help one to unwind. Last night, I lectured on the art of relaxation, and after nodding in total agreement, he went to the local bookstore and returned with a Sand Castle Manual. This morning, he left at 7 and went to Ace Hardware. He proudly appeared on the beach with a shovel, a saw, two trowels, a very large plastic garbage can, a medium-sized one, and various castle molds.

To say this fellow is intense would be … accurate. A family of five—who have been close friends for many years—joined us at the beach for week two. Frank put everybody to work—except for the two women (he didn't dare). He assigned specific tasks to his friend and to all six children. By noontime, the joy was gone. The kids revolted. They were groaning and whining and whispering to one another about which definition of child abuse would hold up in court. Frank fired our friend's children and doubled the workload for ours. My sweet son, Jordan, was the water mule, and his shoulders were sagging. Capri had to keep the entire structure moist with a spray bottle. Paris was told to keep digging.

Frank straddled the middle of the worksite like Yul Brenner; alternately digging and barking orders and planning the next architectural detail. I basked and he multi-tasked. Jordan approached my chair with deep emotion. He begged me to set him free. Our friend's daughter labeled Frank a tyrant, and I insisted on a swimming break before lunch. The children were so grateful.

We ate a deli lunch on the beach, and in the four hours that followed, Frank kept working. I asked him to rest every hour or so, and he insisted his project *was* bringing him rest. We all rolled our eyes. (Yes, yes, I know it's a sin.) The kids came and went according to their capacity to take orders in the heat. Body surfing, kite flying, and ball throwing were welcome diversions to Frank's idea of resting. As certain worker bees dropped off, fate had it that people sitting near or walking by would sign on for brief assignments. Frank was so pleased to have Supreme Court Justice Rehnquist's Chief of Staff at his side, lifting the heavy load for the castle tower. I would have arranged a private tour back at The Court—not Frank. He is not one to mix business and pleasure.

He is focused. He is determined. He is a man deeply committed to his rest.

He is also a head case. Who, in their right mind, would work all day in the hot sun with shovels, trowels, and saws in order to relax? Frank Lofaro, that's who. And you know what? By the end of the day, Frank and his reluctant assistants had built the most impressive sandcastle I've ever seen—replete with turrets, arched windows, and a double moat. I hadn't seen Jordan look that proud since the day he potty trained. Vacationers were stopping, staring, and taking pictures. My very tanned and tired husband tried to remain humble. I grabbed my camera, and as I snapped away, I noted the joy in Frank's face. Once again he had found rest in his "work." During that perfect time that comes at the close of a beach day, we watched as the deep moat and the high wall stood up to the tide. Frank packed up his tools and we all left the beach at 7.

The world has yet to see what God will do with, and for, and through, and in, and by the man who is fully and wholly consecrated in Him. I will try my utmost to be that man.

—D.L. Moody

Lord, make all you can make of my life.

—David C. Cook

T hen I heard the voice of the Lord saying, "Whom shall I send? And who will go for us?" And I said, "Here am I. Send me!"

—Isaiah 6:8

23

All You Need Is Love

You know how the song goes. It's the same as all the other love songs. What the world needs now. Love is always the answer. Love will keep us together. Love makes the world go 'round. All you need is love. Sounds wonderful until reality hits. Our definitions, expressions, and expectations of love are so varied. Human love is highly flawed because, um, well—it's human.

Jesus stated that the greatest expression of love is to lay down one's life for another. I used to think He was referring to the fiery stake, the coliseum, or the foxhole. That's awfully convenient thinking for a woman living in tree-lined suburbia. It has taken twenty years of marriage, fifteen years of motherhood, thirty years of Christianity, and countless relationships—but I have finally begun to grasp what "laying down one's life" looks like.

Unfortunately, comprehension does not always produce desired behavior. The apostle Paul made that quite clear. (I do, I don't, I want, I can't …) My love is finite and not always kind (ask Frank). My love is often impatient and prone to outbursts of frustration (ask my kids). My love takes offense and keeps a record of wrongs (ask my friends). My love is often self-seeking and does not naturally look to wash the feet of others (ask my pastor). And as I look around me, I realize I'm not alone. I don't need to visit a war torn country to observe man's inhumanity to man. I can watch it at my own dinner table, during the P.T.A. meeting or at the toy store. Once in a while, it can even be observed in the church lobby.

With due respect to the modern oracles of popular culture, the mantra "I will love who I want, when I want, in the way I want" just doesn't cut the mustard. A recent magazine article quoted a popular female icon on her disdain for always doing what other people expect her to do. She contended that she would no longer do anything, or go anywhere, or care for anyone unless she wanted to.

Unless she wants to? So much for denying one's self, picking up the cross, and decreasing so God can increase. I suppose it's for the best that Oprah doesn't have kids. I can't say changing diapers, standing on sidelines in drizzle, or driving in circles all day are tasks I want to do. The duties and sacrifices involved in marriage also require a large dose of selflessness. And true friendship that is not self-seeking is hard to find and harder to maintain. You're wealthy if you have found one true friendship.

So where is genuine love to be found? Isn't that what most people say they're searching for? Reality television, psychic hotlines, personal ads, and the like are all straws in the futile grasp to reach Nirvana. If, as a Christian, your heart, does not break for those who have felt shortchanged in the economy of pure, true love then maybe you need a heart transplant. May the Lord have mercy on believers who have ceased to be merciful. I am far from being an expert in matters of the heart and I do not claim to be one who always loves purely, but I do know where to go to find this ever elusive, often fabled, poorly imitated treasure called love. I have discovered a deep well that never runs dry, and it is my thrill (as well as my purpose in life) to tell others where to find it.

Look out the window, down the office hall, into the next car, and around your kitchen table. There are a lot of love-starved people nearby. You may be one of them. Hurting hearts abound, and there are many imposters who are more than happy to step up and wreak havoc on these fragile lives. Sure, there have always been false prophets at every turn, but there has also always been a remnant of God's people who refuse to be silent about "the well." How grateful I am for the cup bearers, the torch carriers, the prayer warriors, and the burden sharers. They are not many in number, but they are mighty in stature. I took a lifetime membership with this group just a few years ago. The dues are quite high, but the perks are fabulous. I am learning what real love is, and I will never again settle for cheap imitations.

Turn to the very familiar but infrequently modeled "love passage" in 1 Corinthians 13. Read it. Read it again, and substitute the name Jesus for the word love. Encouraged? Jesus is synonymous with love. Read it a third time, and substitute your own name for the word love. Discouraged? Don't be. You have the rest of your life to become a great lover of God and of people. God's love is absolutely perfect because, um, well, He's God.

So, send out those Valentine cards and give flowers to special people while they are still on this earth. Sing your favorite love song, enjoy a piece of chocolate, and allow your heart to smile. And don't forget to tell everybody where that amazing well is and what it holds. After all, what the world needs now is Jesus, sweet Jesus. Jesus is always the answer. Jesus will keep us together. Jesus makes the world go 'round. All you need is Jesus.

W hoever drinks of the water that I shall give him will never thirst. But the water that I will give him will become in him a well of water springing up into everlasting life.

—John 4:14 (NKJV)

24

The Company of Women

I truly enjoy the company of women, and I absolutely cherish the fellowship of women who love God, so you can imagine how blessed I am to be afforded the privilege of traveling around the country addressing "soul sisters." Whether I speak at a weekend retreat, a one day conference, or a dinner banquet, I always marvel at the incredible talents and testimonies of so many lovely ladies. In the words of Patsy Clairmont, "I love being a woman!"

A consistent bit of feedback I receive from Women's Ministry directors and pastors is that I seem to genuinely enjoy myself at these various gatherings. I always take my camera along and arrive back home with Kodak memories. At banquets, I visit each table as if I'm the bride. At retreats, I stay up late and walk around in my pajamas in search of chocolate or munchies. I seek out the "golden girls" and ask them questions about life and what it's like to know Jesus for sixty or seventy years. Clearly, I am an extrovert.

One time, I found myself "assigned" to a role in an impromptu skit that resulted in the placement of an undergarment atop my head. At one retreat, I spoke at a podium next to a five-foot-tall pink flamingo for all four sessions. (Those California girls are so wild and crazy.) One time, I led a congo line of women in nightgowns shouting out the lyrics to "When the Saints Go Marching In." (You know they're from New York.) One time, I made believe I knew sign language, and I signed as the entire group locked arms, swayed, and crooned "Edelweiss," a healing experience for everyone in the room. (Just love those Presbyterians from Virginia.) One time, I agreed to hike up a mountain during Saturday afternoon free time, and the leader of the hike brought a roll of toilet paper along. They weren't kidding. (God bless those healthy Coloradoans.) At a predominantly African American church, I fulfilled my dream of being Diana Ross as two lovely "Supremes" flanked my sides. We sang a praise chorus "in the Motown way" and, Oh Lordy, we all had a glorious taste of the heavenly places.

At a retreat of 1,000 women, the fire alarm went off in the middle of the night and we all jumped out of bed, into elevators, and onto the grounds of the Marriott Resort, which was filled to capacity. At least a dozen came "near" to see what the speaker wears to bed. That was humbling. Two senior saints passed me on the way back to the room and whispered (a bit loudly), "Her hair stays in place," to which her friend promptly replied, "Looks too neat. Maybe it's a wig."

Sometimes, the worship team sounds professional and I later find out they are (Go, Nashville!). Sometimes, there are three generations present and the granddaughters are friends, and their mothers are friends, and their grandmothers have been friends since time began. (We all need more of what Ohio has). Sometimes, women send me "recipes for dummies" when I explain I can't cook. (Nothin' could be finer than the meals in Carolina!). Those recipes have literally saved my (domestic) life. So many great memories, so much laughter, so much joy. But that's just half of it.

There is an awful lot of pain in this world. Some people's stories are horribly tragic. Their losses are heart wrenching. Their testimonies are touching. Their courage is inspiring. Their resolve to love and serve God in the midst of carrying a cross quiets me. Box office hits and best selling novels pale in comparison to the firsthand accounts of what God has brought these precious souls through. I am deeply impacted by the heroic women I've met along the way.

Janie has two sons, 8 and 11. In a 6 month period, both were diagnosed with a rare form of cancer.

Doris has a husband with advanced paralytic arthritis and a mother in early stages of Alzheimer's. She has no children and is their sole caretaker.

Wanda had been in the streets for as long as she could remember. She was dealing and prostituting by age 14. She is now 36, married to a godly man, and is HIV positive.

Lou Ann's husband has just been given a twelve-year prison sentence for a white collar crime. She has four children; the oldest is 7.

Marie had three abortions before giving her life to God. Now happily married, she longs to have a family but has been unable to conceive.

Anita was sexually molested by her father for 8 years. The abuse ended 10 years ago but she finds it very hard to go home for the holidays. Her mother has a broken heart.

Diane has been battling manic depression for over twenty years and sometimes fears she will lose her mind. She has finally coming to terms with her need for medication.

Susan's husband is a well-liked pastor addicted to internet pornography. He has convinced her that if it is made known, the entire congregation will be destroyed.

Elizabeth has battled breast cancer for 7 years with several seasons of victory. It has now spread to her organs. She has been given 3 to 6 months to live. She has three teenagers.

Barbara runs a dynamic women's ministry for a mega church. She loves her job and hates her body. She finds herself using food as a pain killer and has entered counseling.

So, what do they all have in common? Each of these women (not their real names) are dealing with serious trials in the present.

Each of them face hardship on a daily basis. Each of them has a reason to be bitter, to give up, to succumb to the weight of their burdens.

Why are they heroic? They have chosen the narrow road called Christianity. They have found life, hope, healing, and a future in the arms of Jesus. They have placed their worries and sorrows at the foot of the cross. They are well acquainted with grief and yet maintain a deep devotion to a Savior familiar with the depths of despair, treachery, rejection, and abandonment. They know He died for them and that gives them reason to live. They press on, they are resolute, they seek God each day, and each day, He meets them. They have found His promises to be true. In Him, they find rest and yes, even joy, in the midst of life's sorrows. And that's the whole of it.

> T he name of the LORD is a strong tower; the righteous run to it and are safe.
>
> —Proverbs 18:10

25

Diary of a Sad Housewife

Thursday, October 3

I was busy finalizing my notes for a keynote dinner address to be given the following evening. I was pleased not to have to fly out for the weekend since the church was only 45 minutes away. My eyes kept glancing at the clock, as they do every weekday afternoon, since I must leave at 3:00 sharp to pick up Jordan from his Christian school 15 miles away. At 2:00 the phone rang and it was Jordan. He wanted to know if I heard the news. Since I do not watch TV during the week or listen to the radio except while driving, I had not heard any news. He informed me that five people had been shot and killed in Maryland and that a madman was on the loose. I informed him I would be prompt and reminded him of his Strength and Shield.

Friday, October 4

The morning paper reported a sixth person was shot the night before and that a pattern had been established. Some witnesses noticed a white van in the vicinity of the shootings. All victims were struck by a single bullet. All were going about daily routines. All were loved by family and friends. The names and faces and stories of all six victims were printed. The faces touched me, moved me, haunted me. More lives ended. More dreams crushed.

More questions. More unanswered "whys." The faces....

The program analyst was leaving Shoppers Food Warehouse with groceries for a church event. The landscaper was mowing the lawn of an auto dealership, as he had for ten years. The cabdriver from India was fueling up to get home to celebrate his twenty-fifth wedding anniversary. The former law student was sitting on a bench reading a book, waiting for a ride to work. The nanny from Idaho was vacuuming her car. The handyman from Haiti stood at a corner while running errands for his invalid wife.

I tended to my own errands, chores, carpools—the usual "To Do List." At 5:00, I showered, dressed, grabbed my notes and my Bible and headed north on the Beltway toward Silver Spring, Maryland. I was well aware that four of the victims had resided in that town. The 45 minute drive took twice as long in rush hour and I had never noticed so many white vans in my life. Traffic crawled while my imagination sped on. I used the time to make a few calls. One well-meaning relative suggested I "stay far away from Maryland where that nut is shooting people." I informed her that the banquet (which I agreed to attend four months earlier) was at a church in the middle of the trouble and that it was a privilege to bring words of hope and healing to the women there. Her reply did not share quite the same sentiment.

I called the event coordinator to assure her I was making slow but steady progress. I told her I understood if the attendance was drastically affected in light of the events. No doubt people would be staying close to home, afraid to venture out for a church event. She told me the events had caused the dinner to have overflow seating. It was record attendance.

When I finally arrived, the parking lot was indeed full and I ended up parking behind the building in an area which was sparsely lit. I took a deep breath, adjusted my lipstick, turned off my cell phone, grabbed my briefcase and experienced cardiac arrest as a white van slowly pulled up and the headlights shone on me. Two men were in it and I became one with the floor of my SUV. I said a brief prayer, ("OH JESUS!") and groped for my cell phone, which I failed to locate. The headlights remained on my vehicle for another 30 seconds and my heart rate accelerated with each one. The van drove away slowly and I sprinted to the entrance. Their speaker had finally arrived—the woman bearing the message of God's faithfulness had entered the building. The Women's Ministry Director greeted me as I spoke in a high, breathless pitch; arms flailing. I informed her that a white van was circling the parking lot. Sighing, she hugged me and was quick to explain that the white vehicle was the "beefed up" church security van manned by husbands of committee women.

Saturday, October 5

I learned a woman had been shot in the back as she left a Michael's craft store in Virginia. She did not die. I imagined she had bought items to make a home or classroom festive for the fall season. My 15-year-old daughter Paris and I stopped at Toys R Us that afternoon for several gifts. It was in a shopping center next to a different Michael's but I "quizzed" her on what she would do if the unthinkable were to happen. I was somewhat comforted when she answered that if there *should* be a gunshot and if I *should* suddenly drop to the ground, she would run (hopefully she would check for a pulse first). Then I reminded her of our citizenship in a timeless Kingdom and assured her that nothing could separate us from God or from one another.

Sunday, October 6

After church, we picked up fresh bagels and headed home. It was a rainy, dreary, sweats and jeans, stay inside day. The *Sunday Washington Post* detailed the shootings and the personal stories connected to each victim. More faces—more broken hearts.

Monday, October 7

Just after 8 A.M., a 13 year old boy was shot in the abdomen as he reached for the front door of his middle school. His concerned aunt didn't want him taking the bus so she made the effort to personally drive him. She watched as he dropped to the ground. My son Jordan is 13. Every mother of every child within an hour of that school was on the phone that morning. Our county declared a Code Blue Alert. No walkers, no outdoor recess, no crossing guards, no after-school activities, no community sports.

Frank was out of town, so I decided to treat the kids to a gourmet dinner at Wendy's. We shared our thoughts and our fears and our faith. I reminded the children of our good and strong foundation in Christ. The two teenagers reminded me that several of the victims were substantial believers. I did not respond with quick, hollow, or pat explanations. When I tucked in our daughter Capri, she informed me she has had a sad year. She hopes being 11 will be much better than being 10.

I watched the 11:00 news and learned the vehicle in question is a white box truck. There are 14,000 of them in the D.C. metro area. A tarot card was found near the middle school with the message "I am God" written on it. Satan has been a pathetic imposter since Eve bit that apple. The boy who was gunned down by the sniper that morning is a well-liked honor roll student. The bullet entered his abdomen, traveled upward and lodged just below his heart. The doctors removed his spleen and parts of his stomach and pancreas. He is in critical condition and on a ventilator. God didn't do that. God loves that boy.

God won't be mocked.

Wednesday, October 9

An engineer who was widowed two years earlier after 27 years of marriage was killed at a gas station just 20 minutes from our home. His brother explained, "When Dean's wife died, he could take one of two paths. He could be bitter and angry at the cruel loss (she was killed by a drunk driver) or he could trust in God. Being a man of faith, he chose the latter." Now the extended family decided they would do the same. "You've got to decide whether you are going to be bitter and angry against God or you're going to believe that God is big enough and strong enough and powerful enough that he knows what's going on. We just have to trust the Lord. We are thankful for our time with Dean—we've been so privileged to know and love him."

Friday, October 11

I drove Capri to school at 9:15 and went straight to a local

Exxon station to have our Durango inspected. I idled on line a while, and by 10 I was waved into the garage and then out of the driver's seat. In the waiting room, a special news bulletin came across a TV suspended from a bracket on the wall. It stated that yet another victim had been felled. At 9:30 A.M., a man was shot while standing at the pump of an Exxon station in Virginia. I later learned that he was a father of six who had finished his business trip and was about to head home to Philadelphia for a restful weekend. Through his cell phone, his wife had just reminded him to be careful.

Saturday, October 12

Code Blue Alert continues. Capri's soccer game has been cancelled this morning, and the same goes for Jordan's football game tonight. The children have described practice drills at school where the teacher barricades the door and they huddle under their desks. In ten days, ten innocent people have been shot. Eight have died and two are struggling to hang on to life.

I am a transplanted New Yorker living in the Washington suburbs. My heart was broken by the events of September 11, but this is very different. This brand of terrorism is daily, unpredictable, relentless, elusive, terrifying, brazen, indiscriminate. This feels like a hunt, a sadistic game, a test of our courage. Fear lurks just under our actions, thoughts, and words. It's a reasonable fear. One that causes you to look around more, to get in your car while the gas is pumping, to keep moving in open spaces. And for believers, it's a fear that ultimately directs us to the sovereign plan and perfect provision of a loving God.

Monday, October 14

We picked pumpkins today and thanked God that Christopher Columbus believed in what he could not see. A sweet day turned sour when the newscaster announced that a woman was shot dead loading her Home Depot purchases into her car at 9:15 tonight. She was recovering from a double mastectomy. It was the first sniper shooting in the county where we live, just a couple of towns away. Nine dead.

Tuesday, October 15

As I write this, the sniper is still roaming and looking to devour. I know God can stop him, and I also know God's ways are higher than mine. I have many unanswered questions about what God "allows" and why, yet I am powerless in attaining answers. Now I see dimly, but one day, I will see clearly and understand the things that remain hidden on this side of heaven. Until that glorious day, I pray for courage, for resolve, for renewed passion, for an evangelical heart, and for bold conviction to say without flinching that, **"For me, to live is Christ ... and to die is gain."** Scripture states that in the last days, hearts would faint with fear. That passage has become much clearer this past year. God help us to stand.

> You will keep in perfect peace him whose mind is steadfast, because he trusts in you.
> —Isaiah 26:3

26

King of Hearts

I enjoy Louis Armstrong's rendition of "A Wonderful World." And every Thanksgiving weekend, my family gathers round to kick off the holiday season as we view our "colorized version" of Frank Capra's "It's A Wonderful Life." And I absolutely love Roberto Begnini's "Life is Beautiful." I believe it *really* is.

Sometimes.

I was tucking the baby into bed the other night (she's ten). It was a very cold night, heralding the onset of winter, and we went through our usual rituals. After I planted the last kiss on her forehead and headed toward the door, she startled me with a comment that caused my footsteps to shift into automatic reverse.

"Mommy, it hasn't been a very good year."

"Capri, what do you mean?"

"Well, I couldn't wait to turn double digits, but it's not goin' too great."

"Is something wrong at school? Is someone bothering you?"

"No, Mom! School is fine. Something is wrong with *the world.*"

"Can you tell me what's wrong? I love you so much. Maybe we can fix it."

"*Everything's* wrong Mom! It has been a very bad year. First the Twin Towers, then the Pentagon, then the anthrax, then Iraq, then the snipers. Those bad men came so close to our house. I think it's a *terrible* world. I hope being eleven is much better than being ten."

My heart sank and my head dipped and my suddenly weak frame slipped softly onto her bed. As is my recent custom, I attempted to be a good listener and I tried not to respond too quickly. No cheap answers. No band-aids. No hurling of Christian clichés. My child was obviously hurting, and I was mindful of Jesus' admonition to mourn with those who mourn.

Three unsettling weeks in October 2002 will always be remembered as a time when fear made its home in and around the Beltway. The sniper shootings terrorized our communities and it was all so very personal. Our children's sports schedules were cancelled, as was outdoor recess. The schools held emergency drills, many people stayed inside, and gas tanks were only filled when necessary. One night, Capri and I sprinted from the door of a Home Depot to our car. I pretended it was a game, in much the same way that the father in Begnini's masterpiece turned the instructions of Hitler's SS into a charade so that his young son Joshua would not comprehend the severity of their Nazi imprisonment.

Capri's face looked so sad as she turned toward the nightlight. I snuggled up close and I "spooned" her from behind. My thoughts drifted to the days when we could take off on our banana bikes early in the morning and not come home until dinner. That is, except for PB&J sandwiches, dimes for the ice cream man, and first aid for bruised knees. When we got thirsty, we drank water from somebody's garden hose.

We built go-carts and stilts and played dodge ball until we were bruised. We got cuts and broken bones and chipped teeth, and nobody got sued. We had shoeboxes full of baseball cards and we "flipped" and "called Larry's" until the winner took all. The losers rarely cried, and parents never got involved in our squabbles. My brothers were always "wiping out" on their friends' mini-bikes (we weren't allowed to own one), and we spent endless hours during both summer and winter down at the neighborhood pond. We never caught any diseases there, even though we touched many unnamed slimy things.

Forty years have passed. A generation. How could our lives have changed so much? My ten year old feels she has had a bad year.

And it's not about a mean classmate or a teacher who gives a lot of homework. She thinks it's a terrible world because she has felt the personal effects of political turmoil. She is a young American and sadly, she is reminded fairly consistently that there are an awful lot of bad people out there—and now in here—in our own backyard. Her teenage brother and sister have experienced much of the same, but they are better equipped to articulate their feelings and to sort through "the real vs. the felt" threat to their safety and well being. I petitioned God for guidance and took a deep breath.

"Capri—I think you're right. The world has been out of control lately. But really, it's always been out of control, and that's exactly why Jesus came to this world. He wanted to help us and to give us hope and to remind us that our life on earth is not the end of the line. As a matter of fact, it's only the beginning."

"Mommy, I know Jesus loves us and I know we're goin' to heaven and I know you always say you'll meet me at the gate; but that's a long time away for me."

"We're not going to be happy and safe just when we live in heaven. Jesus came as the best Christmas present ever to give us happiness and safety right now. We don't have to be afraid. We are so safe in the hands of God."

"Well, it doesn't feel very safe to me. Maybe God's mad."

"No, baby girl. God is sad. He gave His only Son to show us how to live, and most people ignore Him. A lot of people don't even think of Him on His birthday, but He is still God, and He is *always* good. When you asked Jesus to live in your heart, you got a whole lot of presents all at once. Maybe we could go over that list sometime, so you can be reminded of what He gave you. You know, you're the daughter of a King, so that makes you a Princess! Princesses have a lot of stuff!"

"You mean Nintendo, Playstation, and X Box?" She smirked knowingly.

"No, silly goose. I mean she is safe and she knows the King is always protecting her and she understands that the King is going to let her live forever and ever in a place with no tears or fears or sadness. It's the happiest ending there ever was, and the best part is that it never ends. Also, the Princess gets to be joyful and peaceful right from the beginning cause she knows the King's in charge. And she knows He loves her. And she loves Him."

"I get it Mom."

"Good. Go to sleep."

"I will if you stop breathing in my ear."

"Sorry. Good night."

"Mom, don't forget—basketball starts tomorrow. I got pretty good at camp. It's gonna be a great time. I can't wait to play. Wait till the coach sees me dribble."

I lifted my tired body and kissed her once more and headed down the hallway.

God didn't send His only Son on that first Christmas long ago to be a tenant or a landlord in our hearts. He came to establish His Kingdom in each one of us. With Jesus as King of Hearts—it **really is** a wonderful world.

"We are not citizens of this world trying to make our way to heaven. We are citizens of heaven trying to make our way through this world. There is nothing we can lose on earth that can rob us of the treasure God has given us and will give us."
—The Anglican Digest

For he has rescued us from the dominion of darkness and brought us into the kingdom of the Son he loves, in whom we have redemption, the forgiveness of sins.
—Colossians 1:13–14

27

To Sirs, with Love

Tina Turner is wrong about many things. That said, I like her spunk, her raspy voice, and her determination to "live again" after almost dying in an abusive marriage. Ms. Turner is sixty-something; all the more reason for one to take note of her career longevity and those amazing legs. Her jaded stance on love and romance is understandable considering her past, but she really misses the mark when she croons "We don't need another hero." Actually, we could use some real heroes. As I look at our culture, I am disheartened by the condition of our hero roster.

Calm down and don't be so quick to point to the second commandment. I'm not referring to idols. I'm talking about heroes. Big difference. Without God at the center of one's life, just about everyone and everything is a candidate for idolatry. This month a person, next month a car, your reputation, your education, your denomination, your child—you know how it works. Conversely, having Almighty God as one's reason for existence produces values and priorities in keeping with His ways. The Bible is full of stories about people whose behavior God wants us to emulate … or avoid. It offers accounts of heroes and idols—good guys and bad guys—role models and "don't go there" models. And Scripture is very clear about delineating the Who's Who Lists. There is no guesswork.

Of course, heroes make mistakes—they're only human. I am

not suggesting believers don't stumble. I brush dirt off my hands and knees on a regular basis. A medieval monk penned, "A saint is just a sinner who falls down but gets up." I would like to offer an addendum: "A hero is just a sinner who acts more like a saint with each passing year."

Unlike many females, I am enjoying the aging process. I am not thrilled about gravity's victory over my body parts, but I rejoice because of the progress of my unseen parts. I rejoice that I'm not who I was, and I am humbled since I'm not quite who He's making me to be. When you spend a great deal of time in an intimate relationship, you begin to take on the character traits, mannerisms, and inflections of your loved one. So it is for those who walk and talk with God. We should be growing in spiritual stature. God does not intend for us to be stunted but Satan does, and sidetracking believers is a popular tactic in the war room of hell.

We all need to assess our development. Politicians love to ask if you are better off than you were four years ago. King Jesus would like you to answer that same question in a spiritual context. Well, are you? There are some who are quick to award themselves straight As. Beware of the boasters. As I grow older, I find myself drawn to the heroes of the faith who, like Paul, are painfully aware of the hopelesssness of their own weakness were it not for the grace and forgiveness found at Calvary. His mercies are new every morning.

I attended the 25th Anniversary celebration of Prison Fellowship Ministries. We heard testimony after testimony of how Chuck's conversion to Christ was likened to that of the apostle Paul. Charles W. Colson served a seven month prison sentence for his role in the Watergate scandal. It seemed as though Mr. Colson had gained the world and lost his soul. But God had other plans. A year to the day after being released, Prison Fellowship was established. A quarter century later, the ministry is the largest of its kind, touching hundreds of thousands of lives in over 90 countries. Chuck Colson commented that in actuality, he was given a *life* sentence—prison is where his heart remains.

This year, Chuck Colson's good friend Dr. James Dobson will celebrate the 25th Anniversary of Focus on the Family. The radio broadcasts, books, teaching tapes, magazines, and other resources produced by this ministry touch lives on every continent of the earth. I am so grateful that this pediatric psychologist from southern California decided to take a leap of faith that has produced ripple effects we will never fully measure in this lifetime or on this planet.

Neither Chuck Colson nor Jim Dobson will probably ever be chosen as *Time* magazine's "Man of the Year." They are not likely to ever win the Nobel Peace Prize. They certainly won't appear in the history texts. Even so ... they are my heroes. Each has had a profound influence on my life. My broad world-view as well as my personal life skills have been radically affected by the light that each of these fine men have shed on my path. My role as wife, mother, sister, daughter, friend, neighbor, worshiper, and citizen have been directly impacted by their contributions and sacrifices.

Recently I spoke at a youth assembly and posed the following question to the students: If you could choose any person in the world to have dinner with, who would you choose? The girls rattled off names of movie stars, rappers, and cute guys from school. The guys had other criteria. I won't discourage you by listing their top choices ... but let's just say we definitely need more heroes. Where will they come from? Daily, God is building them in your home and mine. The pattern is in God's Word (see Hebrews 11), and the world is waiting and watching.

Therefore, since we are surrounded by such a great cloud of witnesses, let us throw off everything that hinders and the sin that so easily entangles, and let us run with perseverance the race marked out for us. Let us fix our eyes on Jesus, the author and perfecter of our faith, who for the joy set before him endured the cross, scorning its shame, and sat down at the right hand of the throne of God.

—Hebrews 12:1–2

28

Three Sons

Death is difficult. I don't fear it, but I can't honestly say I embrace it. Politically correct Christians say they can't wait to go to heaven. Not me. Heaven can wait. I have a lot to do here on earth. Conceptually, I feel a peace about it, but I do have normal concerns about my final exit. Will my own death be painful and drawn out? Will I go to sleep one night and sail right on through the pearly gates? My gene pool suggests I will leave this planet due to cardiac failure. That does not seem as horrific as suffering with a lingering disease, but the rapture of a chocolate overdose would be preferable to all other scenarios. For now, I'm pursuing life to the fullest, and I will go on doing so until it comes. And death will come. Each one of us has an appointment with it—make no mistake. (I dare you to find a living, prosperity-preaching faith healer born before 1920.)

During the weeks before Christmas I wear a pin that says "Happy Birthday Jesus!" It sparks a lot of interesting conversations—especially at check-out counters. During the weeks before Easter I wear a pin that says "Born once, die twice. Born twice, die once." That one gets even more responses than my Christmas pin. The conversations immediately expose people's theology (or lack thereof). There is an awful lot of misinformation out there. In the words of my wise husband, "information is power." Many are obviously missing some key information about Jesus Christ.

Jesus said "I am the way, the truth, and the life." Notice that He didn't claim to be "a way," but rather, "THE way." What a difference a word makes! Jesus is THE way. I cringe when some affirm His goodness, wisdom, and morality, but then deny His deity. These are the people who compare Jesus to Mohammed, Buddha, Moses, and Gandhi. To be sure, there were noble traits in each of these men. But in the final analysis, they were all just that … mere men. Jesus Christ claimed to be God. That's why they killed Him. How good was Jesus if He told lies and allowed His disciples, the early church, and countless millions to die for a myth? How wise was Jesus to submit to a painful death if there was no hope of resurrected life? How moral was Jesus if He led His followers astray—if He knowingly promised "a place in my Father's house" and there was nothing behind that promise?

I am saddened as well as deeply sympathetic with people who are angry with God because of the loss of a loved one. Where was He? How could He? Why didn't He? For these tortured souls, the questions are endless and often go unanswered. They will not be comforted if they will not seek the Comforter. I am taken aback by the people who insist that this life is hell. They will not be enlightened because they will not turn toward the Light of the World. Then there are those who are confident that except for Herod, Hitler, and Hussein—we are all going to heaven. After all, isn't that where good people go? They don't know the truth because they do not know the One Who is Truth.

Maggie had been attending my neighborhood Bible study for about a year and she had e-mailed me with the words "I finally get it." I knew what she meant and God knew what she meant, and I knew the angels were having a grand celebration in heaven. In February of 2001, my friend Maggie awoke on a Saturday morning to find her sweet little boy's lifeless body in his bed. In disbelief, she carried Cory (who was about to turn three) to the master bedroom where she and her husband Rick applied CPR and prayer. Both seemed to be futile. I wondered what those same angels were doing that Saturday afternoon as Cory's body laid in the office of the medical examiner.

Four days later, I spoke at the funeral and reminded family and friends of the great promise of the One (the only one) who conquered sin and death. The tiny casket that sat between the altar and the front pew brought many questions to the hearts and minds of each person in that church. It's hard enough to be near any casket—but this one was so little—caskets are not supposed to be so little. After the funeral mass, I hugged Maggie in the lobby. She brought her wet face near mine and whispered, "I don't think I get it."

I reassured her and walked to my car wondering what I "get" about the mysteries of life and death. There is so much that we will never understand on this side of eternity, but I have placed my stake in the ground about the fact that Jesus Christ is the way, the truth, and the life. He is my hope, my strength, and my song. There is no pain or difficulty that He has not taken upon Himself. I am so comforted to know I trust in the God who has gone before me and yet comes alongside me. He is my Savior and my friend.

I glean a great deal from the sermons and books of Chuck Swindoll. Formerly a pastor of a mega-church in southern California, he is now serving as President of the highly esteemed Dallas Theological Seminary. Allow me to share a true story from one of Dr. Swindoll's Easter sermons.[2]

It was 1948. The setting was a small town along the great Mississippi River. The bridge-keeper was responsible to raise the drawbridge to allow boats to pass on the river below and to lower it again for trains to cross over on land. One day, the bridge-keeper's son came along to watch his father at work. Quite curious, as most boys are, he peeked into a trap door that was always left open so his father could keep an eye on the great machinery that raised and lowered the bridge. While the bridge was up, the boy leaned too far forward, lost his balance, and tumbled into the mighty gears. As the father reached down to pull him out, he heard the whistle of an approaching train. He knew the train was full of people and that it was impossible to stop the fast-moving locomotive. The bridge had to be lowered.

What a terrible dilemma to be in—if he saved the passengers, his son would be crushed in the cogs. If he saved his son, hundreds of people would die when the train plowed into the bridge and plunged into the river. Frantically, he tried to reach for his son, but the boy was too far down. Finally, the father put his hand to the lever that would start the machinery. He paused, uttered a loud groan, and with tears streaming down his face, he pulled the lever. The giant gears began to work and the bridge clamped down just in time to save the train. The bridge-keeper saved the passengers' lives at the cost of his own son's.

This heart-wrenching account echoes what was done at Calvary. What an incredibly clear illustration of God's sacrificial love. He, too, let his Son die in order for others to live. God gave His only Son to save you and me. How great His love is to do such a thing! God's son ... Maggie's son ... the bridge-keeper's son. Though they have died—yet they fully live. At times, it is too difficult to grasp, but I am embracing God's promises. Indeed, I will hold on for dear life ... and for death, which will have no sting.

The LORD is a refuge for the oppressed, a stronghold in times of trouble. Those who know your name will trust in you, for you, LORD, have never forsaken those who seek you.

—Psalm 9:9–10

29

Beyond Bonding:
Loving the Blonde Women

Young couples do not generally move away from that grand NYC suburb called Long Island. Old people leave—either for Florida or a cemetery, but not the young ones. New Yorkers complain a lot. The taxes, the stress, the cost of living. Long commutes, short tempers, daily displays of road rage. Yet when all is said and done, the many millions who work, live, and play in and around New York absolutely love it there. And what's not to love? It's the capital of the world and they know it.

I grew up on Long Island, and like the majority of baby boomers from the post WWII era, most of us were born within ten or twenty minutes of the neighborhoods where our grandparents settled after checking their luggage through Ellis Island. A friend recently told me (with great confidence), that one of every four Americans can trace his/her roots back to Brooklyn.

During the wonder years of the sixties, many children of the great wave of early-twentieth-century immigrants moved out of the five boroughs of NY and into the sprawling suburbs. There they pursued the good life, and many attained it. Some of the best beaches in the world, excellent public schools, well-zoned communities, authentic restaurants for every palette, the finest police and fire departments, super malls to upscale shops to fantastic flea markets, skiing in scenic upstate, and the Big Apple are at our fingertips. You can eat and shop any time, and there's delicious pizza by the slice on every corner of every town. And that's just the beginning.

The people are great. Well, okay, some are terrible, but the majority of them are really terrific. Well, okay, a lot of them. Bold, funny, colorful, emotive, generous. Sarcastic, impatient, opinionated, arrogant. Ya gotta love 'em! Have you seen that poster titled "A New Yorker's View of the World." One was given to us nine years ago when we moved away. It has a detailed aerial view of Central Park and the Manhattan skyline as the focal point. Smaller, but still prominent are Brooklyn, Bronx, Queens, Staten Island, Long Island, and Jersey. After the Hudson River, in small print and disproportionate to scale, are a few popular Caribbean Islands, and then a land mass labeled Mexico, South America and Antarctica. That's so funny … well, uh … if you're from New York.

I am from New York, but I no longer live there. We did the thing most New Yorkers never do. We moved away. In 1994, my husband heard God's call to enter Christian ministry, and we moved to a Virginian suburb of Washington, D.C. I wasn't pleased. I wasn't in favor of the move. I never heard the call. But alas, I did the right thing and packed the kids in a Volvo and followed Frank. It's only a five hour drive, but in those first few years, it may as well have been a different planet.

No pizza by the slice, no Carvel ice cream, no restaurants open past 10. (And if they were, they were not worth the trip.) Government gurus and corporate climbers and military men. Big houses and townhouses and garages with remote controls. No stoops or porches to encourage the evening walk or the mid-afternoon chat. No senior citizens and no relatives nearby. Most people are from somewhere else and are passing through. It's a ghost town for the holidays.

Don't pity me. After nine years, I have come to love it here. The pace is just right, Frank now works for a consulting firm 15 minutes away, the people are polite, and I have grown accustomed to chain restaurants. And yes, I have sincerely come to love the blonde women.

As I mentioned earlier, the blonde women in the D.C. area are thin, highly educated, athletic, accessorized, and reserved. I am from an ethnic group that views eating as a sport. The blonde women come dressed up to the school bus stop. I am usually in sweats or pajamas—sans underwear. They blow air kisses and they give air hugs. I am accustomed to greeting people with intentional, full body embraces.

The blonde women all seem to have graduated from interior decorating school. I'm still not sure what to do with potpourri. They raise money for every charity under the sun. I get tired just watching them. They go the gym for pleasure. I get a happy feeling laying down. They show up at every game and cheer their little athletes on to the playoffs. I go to every other game and pray my kids' teams will lose so the nonsense will be over and done with. They all own an SUV or a minivan, and many of them belong to a cult called Creative Memories. My photos have been in shoeboxes under beds for the past twenty years. In New York, people invite you to their home and they feed you delectable treats. The blonde women will meet you for a muffin at a local café.

And no matter how they feel or what they're thinking, they continue to smile and nod. I was always comforted by the New York approach to relational dynamics. You never have to guess where you stand with a true New Yorker.

"Hey! I don't like you … or your mother!"

"Good! 'Cause I never liked your mother!"

After four years of grumbling, murmuring, doing cartwheels for the PTA, serving on (trying to restructure) women's committees, and not really fitting in, I was clearly addressed by that still, small voice of God Almighty one sunny August morning.

Ellie, I want you to love the blonde women.

"Oh no, Lord! Not the blonde women! Ask me anything else. I'll visit prisoners. I'll go back to work in the cafeteria. I'll volunteer at a homeless shelter. Just don't make me be friends with the blonde women!!!"

At the time, I had been a "Capital C Christian" for twenty-five years, and I knew better than to argue with God. The next day, I knocked on every door in my neighborhood and invited each and every woman to a "fun, stimulating, no pressure Bible study." Thirty-three women were invited, and in September of 1998, three of them came. They were blonde. They were thin. They were beautiful. They were smart. They were staring at me. I was thirty pounds overweight and feeling a bit foolish. How could I explain a faith that helps us to be conquerors when I hadn't even addressed my own giants?

If I expected them to take on some of my reading habits, it was clear I needed to learn some of their eating habits. I taught them things about spiritual health, and they taught me a lot about physical health. And they taught me about organization, household management, and how to be quiet even when you don't feel like it.

They entered addresses in my computer and helped me set up filing systems for my teaching materials. They cropped and pasted twenty years of photos into Creative Memories albums. (Of course, the purists thought I was sacrilegious when I refused to journal or add pretty borders.) They gave me recipes, and when that failed they told me where to find great takeout. I just love the blonde women!!!

Most Christian adults would assert they are free from the shackles of prejudice—but are we? Some days we behave like socially-driven, clique-oriented middle-schoolers. I know I have. Maybe like me, you have come to conclusions about others because of what they look like, where they live, how much (or little) they have, and who they mingle with. Maybe you notice what car they drive. Maybe you envy their figure or their house or their spouse. Maybe you work hard to fit in and maybe you work hard to keep your distance. And maybe, like me, you've had it all wrong.

Jesus loves the little children ... and the big ones too.

I'll do better.

F or Christ's love compels us, because we are convinced that one died for all, and therefore all died. And he died for all, that those who live should no longer live for themselves but for him who died for them and was raised again. So from now on we regard no one from a worldly point of view.

—2 Corinthians 5:14–16

Ellie and the blonde women

"I love New York!"

Ellie, Barbara Johnson, and Kathy Troccoli

Capri and Bella Mia Lofaro

My White House moment

*Ellie and
Patsy Clairmont*

The Lofaro Family—Father's Day June 2001

Notes

[1] _____. *Webster's New World Dictionary*, (William Collins Publishers, 1979), p. 476.

[2] Chuck Swindoll. *The Tale of the Tidy Oxcart*, (Word Publishing, 1998), p. 253.

Speaking Engagements

To inquire about having Ellie speak at your event, call or write to:

Ellie Lofaro
PO Box 9292
Reston, VA 20195
Phone/Fax 703.435.5334
Website: www.ellielofaro.com
E-Mail: ellie@ellielofaro.com

The Proverbs 31 Woman
Running the Race of Life
The Gift of Encouragement
Joy in the Journey (Philippians)
Amazing Grace
What Is That In Your Hand?
Dealing with Change
How's Your Love Life? (Corinthians)
The Romance of Ruth
More of You Lord, Less of Me
The "Me" God Sees
Circle of Friends
The Faithfulness of God (Joshua)
A Woman of Prayer
How to Give Away Your Faith
Being a Peacemaker
The Seasons of Life
Discovering Your God-given Gifts
Communication in Marriage
Magnificent Motherhood
Becoming a Whole Woman
Leaving a Legacy
Stress or Rest?
Forgiveness Is for Giving
Sweet Fruits of the Spirit
The Princess Bride
Leaving a Legacy

Specific Requests Are Welcome